ADVANCE PRAISE FOR

Wandering and Welcome

With characteristic agility, Joe Grant invites us to experience the "sacred art of becoming fully human." Through the depth and pace of *Wandering and Welcome* he offers again an immense gift of prayer and poetry, an oasis to nourish and challenge.

—MARIE DENNIS, Pax Christi International

Joe Grant writes and reflects with poetic and prophetic instincts wrapped in words incisive and ponderous. The constellation of scripture verses, compelling quotations, and truthful observations makes this book a resource that you will use over and over again for private and public prayer. Prepare to be unsettled, reminded, refreshed and re-sent.

—JACK JEZREEL, senior advisor, JustFaith Ministries

WANDERING *and* WELCOME

Meditations for Finding Peace

JOSEPH GRANT

franciscan
media
Cincinnati, Ohio

Unless otherwise noted, all scripture quotations have been modified by the author based on the New Revised Standard Version (NRSV) translation.

Quotations from Thomas Merton are used with permission of the Merton Legacy Trust.

Cover and book design by Mark Sullivan
Cataloging in Publication data on file with the Library of Congress.

ISBN 978-1-63253-296-1

Published by Franciscan Media
28 W. Liberty St.
Cincinnati, OH 45202
www.FranciscanMedia.org

Printed in the United States of America.
Printed on acid-free paper.
19 20 21 22 23   5 4 3 2 1

More love, more love,

Alone by its power

The world we will conquer…

—traditional Shaker hymn

I dedicate this collection of reflections to my family:
my wife, Anne, and my three wonderful children,
Brendan, Fiona, and Aidan, who continue to
squeeze more love out of me than I ever
imagined I could contain.

Contents

Acknowledgments

I wish to express my gratitude to the many contributors and participants of the JustFaith Ministries *EngagingSpirituality* process and the
multitude of retreats and presentations that inspired the reflections
at the heart of this book. Particular thanks for the generous support
and generative friendship of Jackie and Bill Brennan, Linda and
Ed Boenisch, Renee and Tim McCarthy, as well as the St. William
Peacemaking Community in Louisville, Kentucky.

A Word to the Wise

On the sabbath he started teaching in the synagogue, and many who heard him were astonished. "Where did this person get all this?," they asked. "What is this wisdom that has been given him?" —MARK 6:2

Dear Seeker,

I address you in this way because, in your own quest for wholeness, this little book of reflections has somehow found you.

Whether you call yourself Christian or whether you follow another path or none in particular, by virtue of having lived some, loved deeply, and lost much, and by the depth of your own soul-searching, you will already be familiar with many of the insights that await you here. Turning these pages may feel like reconnecting with old friends, as you come across well-worn wisdom that is well known to you.

In this instance, *knowing* does not refer to the accumulation of information. In growing deeper and wider, it is important to learn, in so far as we can, to move beyond the congested confines of our heads. The most inscrutable truths of our lives we feel in the bones of our being. So, as you make your own meandering way, slowly—back and forth and back again—through these pages, may you be reacquainted, pleasantly and even perhaps unpleasantly, with unreasonable wisdom that has guided you along the way to this particular bend in the confluence of our lives.

Listen, Learn, Live!

"O Israel, listen: The Most Holy is one; you shall love this Holy One with all heart, with all soul, with all mind, and with all strength"... "You shall love your neighbor as yourself. No other commandment is greater than these."—MARK 12:29-31

In some countries, when people are learning to drive a car, they attach a warning plate to their vehicle, signaling to other travelers that the driver is a learner. In several religious traditions, candidates in training to become monks or ministers wear special robes that announce their apprenticeship. Perhaps there is wisdom in adapting this kind of practice as an internal monitor to warn others and remind ourselves that, in life, we are all always learners. This kind of wisdom inevitably makes for a much more interesting, humbling, and forgiving journey.

Seekers, pilgrims, disciples; all are wayfarers who find themselves stumbling along the stony path toward integrity. They are people trying to live into life's lessons by taking hard-earned insights to heart and turning them into habits. Whether they perceive it as troublesome, disturbing, inspiring, or consoling, seekers embrace everyday wisdom by adopting a receptive attitude, cultivating a learning heart, and approaching life as novices, for whom each experience is welcomed anew. In some Buddhist circles this has been called the Beginner's Mind. Christians might simply call it cultivating a disciple's heart.

This internal attitude involves claiming and reclaiming our authentic status as lifelong disciples, perennial pupils—people who are always practicing. After all, those who wish to be guided must first admit to their own unknowing before they can entrust their lives to another, wiser guide. And, rather than attempting to contain or control facts, parse out details, or digest information, disciples choose: to listen attentively, pause regularly, ponder quietly, question honestly; to rest in reflecting and reflect while engaging in social action; to seek guidance regularly and to deliberately let their lives be led by a Presence greater that moves them into currents deeper. All of this might be framed as prayerful engagement or even active contemplation. Wisdom, it seems, always appears to leaven our lives with implications and practical applications, as well as significant responsibilities.

As with any true quest, the questions and insights captured within these pages and echoed in our own stories take us only as far as we allow. It is the depth and honesty of our questions, our hunger for wholeness, and our readiness to be guided beyond familiar and safe surroundings that will draw the wisdom from within and around us to mark out our path.

All of us teach best what we most need to learn. Honest learners are not looking to have their assumptions verified, to be reassured of the rightness of their own ideas, or to parade their rectitude. Authentic learners are always explorers. As far as possible, they try to move out beyond those limits, over and under the divisive barricades and confines that protect us even as they pen us in and keep us apart. In contrast, disciples approach life with a spacious, freer heart, hoping to listen, to learn, and to grow by making room for new appreciations, deeper understandings, as well as worthier questions.

The scope of every life is indeed defined by the questions we choose to live into, and if we are blessed to live long enough, we will inevitably end up shaped like a question mark. Since *quest* is also the start of every *question*, it is questions, not answers, that are the surest guideposts for any journey of faith—which necessarily means moving into the unknowable. Always trust the open, heartfelt question that lays bare the soul to unknowing.

Since all answers are partial and preliminary, be wary of them; the more definitive, the more dangerous. Whether they are simplistic or sophisticated, handle answers with care, for they often reflect and display, for all the world to see, the broad sweep of our ignorance. Perhaps, for this reason, wisdom teachers use stories, ballads, parables, or poems. Such lyrical musings open spaces for fresh appreciations and diverse perspectives. They foster fascination and expose imagination to wider fields of understanding, laced with mystery, which always leads us down and out to face yet another, more penetrating question.

May this little book inspire you to continue open-ended listening, learning, and authentic living.

THE TIMELESS TAPESTRY: A WORD ABOUT WISDOM

Put out into deeper waters and let down your nets for a catch.
—LUKE 5:4

The threads of wisdom tightly woven into the diverse fibers of our religious traditions reflect the seasoning of cultures, communities, struggling souls, and sages across the ages. This network of wisdom-webbing does not belong exclusively to any singular tradition, institution, caste, or class. Indeed, we do not own wisdom; rather, it captivates and entangles us. Unlike laws and rules, wisdom provides nuance and ambiguity, introduces us to mystery, encourages the search for deeper investigation, and is averse to singular interpretation or restrictive, hard-edged regulation. Proposing a listening posture, wisdom allows us to expose our core to a more complex relationship with realities, whose ramifications persistently remain far beyond the reach of our comprehension.

We recognize wisdom because it rings true; it reverberates and resonates with our lived experience. Unlike information, which comes and goes with time and tide, wisdom is a wild, evolving perception, infinitely bigger than us. And, like all things untamable, we might approach, but never quite grasp it, for the currency of wisdom is mystery. Not to be confused with a puzzle or conundrum, mystery is, by definition, utterly unsolvable. Mysteries draw us in, capture and confound, and gift us with humility and awe. To make room for mysterious wisdom, we first must loosen our grip on information by entertaining that more demanding question: *What might this mean?*

Wisdom speaks of and leads to a bigger picture, a deep-seated awareness of wholeness, a sense of oneness, and interconnection. Amid confusion and division, wisdom presents parables and paradoxes to undermine our defensive bulwarks and help us get over ourselves. In this way, it opens the door to other levels of learning. Though we can transcribe teachings, define and decipher certain applications, underline insights, and commit text to memory, these merely help us recall details but do not necessarily lead to understanding and integration.

In contrast to typical methods of memorization, wisdom traditions propose heart-learning: fostering prayerful, attentive presence with a receptive approach to life. This is the opposite of posturing and pretending. Referred to as a "contemplative stance," this attitude is often misplaced as the counterpoint to active engagement in the tending and mending justice-work of ministry. This contemplative attitude is indeed less concerned with rules or resolutions and more inclined toward the motivations of heart. However, it also encompasses a way of doing, a necessary quality of presence-in-action that nourishes, inspires, and moves us toward deeper engagement with the details, dramas, and distresses of living.

Wisdom neither distracts nor liberates us from our responsibility toward the personal and global struggles and troubles of our time. Taking a longer view, offering a wider angle, it lets us hold, behold, and appraise these difficulties differently, motivating us to mine our tribulations for the graces and lessons hidden therein.

A RESOURCE FOR REFLECTING AND SHARING

No one puts new wine into worn wineskins for the wine would burst them and be lost, along with the skins. New wine goes into fresh skins.—MARK 2:22

This compilation of reflections (excerpted and adapted from a personal blog entitled *In the Storm Still*) reflects the distillation of decades of discipling through religious formation and cross-cultural ministry, as well as programs, retreats, and workshops I have developed and offered far and wide. This book is also a companion to a previous collection of my reflections, published by JustFaith Ministries and entitled *Still In the Storm*.

I offer these reflections as help to any seasoned soul or small circle of care-worn companions looking to faithfully and full-heartedly embrace the blessings and blights presented by these times we share.

There are a variety of ways to share a resource like this, in addition to using it for personal enrichment, and perhaps, as a catalyst for prayerful dialogue with a small group. This book is not designed to be read sequentially. Though the seven chapters are loosely arranged into broad categories, some consistent themes echo and resurface at different places. Rather than progressing through all the reflections in a given chapter, consider a more random, serendipitous approach. Leaf through the pages and select a meditation that has an intriguing title or proposes a pertinent question. You might also choose to focus on a single reflection or one chapter for an entire week, returning to questions or phrases that resonate or challenge. Likewise, you could use this book to accompany a personal retreat or frame a group retreat around one of the recurring themes or chapters. You or your group might even select a specific chapter for daily or weekly reflection during the sacred seasons of Advent, Lent, Easter, or Christmastide.

There is method to the meter and form of these short reflections. In contrast to a prosaic format for sharing insights and questions, the lyrical or poetic phrasing invites a deliberately contemplative appraisal that encourages you to revisit each line as you read and reflect. This format can be particularly helpful when reading aloud in the context of small-group dialogue or prayer. The three-line phrases invite you to pause and parse each line as you revisit it. As you read, reflect, and share these meditations, consider the image of a coin tossed into a well that oscillates from side to side, catching sunlight even as it sinks slowly into deeper darkness.

A WORD ABOUT LANGUAGE

...if salt has lost its taste, how can its saltiness be restored?

—MATTHEW 5:13

Words and names give sound, shape, and definition to our perception and experience of reality, particularly when trying to communicate understanding and incomprehension in the face of ultimate mystery. While each of the reflections in this book begins with a short excerpt from one of the four Gospels, and often includes other scriptural references, these reflections are not intended for use as scripture study. Rather, the bible verses serve as stepping-stones, rooting the themes within the broad sweep of the Christian biblical tradition. Additionally, the scripture quotes have very deliberately been slightly amended or re-patterned to convey a more poetic cadence and refresh our connection with well-worn verses that may have lost their saltiness, sounding rote and overly familiar to our ears. All scripture quotations have been modified from the New Revised Standard Version (NRSV) translation.

STILL IN STORMY TIMES

In stillness my soul awaits you alone, O Holy One. —PSALM 62:1

Amid the tumult of these electrically charged, frenzied times, contemplative living does not propose an escape from our very real, practical, and sometimes intractable problems. On the contrary, it suggests a way of being still, while still being in the storms that rage all around and within us. Like sturdy trees that bend with the breeze, wisdom-inspired living offers a deeper mooring for our being and our doing, which allows for movement even as we are deeply rooted. Seasoned by tears of joy and lament, prayer-centered presence invites us to welcome the whole world by drawing it into our heart-center. Here theology mixes with theater and prophetic action with poetry, as walls come tumbling down, making way for wonder, woe, and well-being.

A great windstorm arose, and such waves beat into the boat that it was being swamped. Meanwhile, in the stern, he lay sleeping on a cushion. They woke him up crying, "Teacher, don't you care that we are drowning?" He awoke, rebuked the wind and called out across the waters, "Peace! Be still!"—MARK 4:37-39

Can we be still and still be in the storms that surround us?

Disasters never fail
to move us,
or draw out the best in us.

For who can watch another
person, city, nation
endure devastation

without feeling disturbed,
touched, moved to connect,
and make some effort to alleviate the suffering?

These uniquely human aspirations;
compassion, mercy, forgiveness, justice;
are essential expressions of our God-likeness.

Holy One, you are gracious and merciful, slow to anger, abounding in steadfast love. You are good to all. Your compassion extends over all you have created.—PSALM 145:8-9

Devastations
of nature and lives
grace us with hard-holy questions:

But why do terrible things happen?
Why do the most vulnerable suffer most grievously?
What might happen if we let our lives become entangled with theirs?

As tragedies compound,
we strain to maintain
an attentive, focused response.

Only when the winds die
and waters recede,
does the long journey toward mending begin.

And how can storm-tossed people
sustain hope
without a tsunami of human, moral, and financial support?

Catastrophe unveils
a collective reservoir
of untapped resources.

Indeed, we are stronger,
deeper, more caring
than we imagine.

Yet, we must also confront other,
more insidious, storm-tides;
fearful forces intent on driving and keeping us apart.

Divisive and distracting tempests
of busyness and cynical self-preoccupation
pummel us daily, eroding our capacity to care.

Unchallenged, these influences
send us spinning frenetically,
beyond the reach of compassionate care.

Compassion cries out to be unleashed,
mercy needs to be nurtured,
forgiveness begs for release.

These resolute reflections of our deepest nature
provide generous immunity
against any force determined to pull us apart.

We are made for togetherness. We are made for all the beautiful
things that you and I know. We are made to tell the world that there
are no outsiders.—DESMOND TUTU, *God Has a Dream*

May the disturbing-consoling Spirit
fold us back together
to make of us all a safe haven in the face of the storm.

An incisive verse by Sufi poet Jalāl ad-Dīn Rūmī translates: "Wherever you stand, be the soul of that place." This wisdom is not easy to embrace. It demands a lifetime of wakefulness practice.

Like travelers on a crowded station platform or milling around a bustling terminal, we are pressed to be ever on the move, as though we were only passengers simply passing through. So, we pass our days looking for the next while we overlook the now. And so much wonder and woundedness pass us by or fail to penetrate. How much do we lose each time we try to grab at many things while failing to grasp what is essential?

If this were your last day, hour, minute, or breath, imagine how you might drink in the daylight, taste the twilight, touch the stars, smell the sunshine, delight at songbirds, listen to the look of your loved ones, bow before the sanctity of a stranger, be carried away with astonishment, and be beside yourself with awe at the wonder of it all. Perhaps we engage life in its fullness when we stop asking if we are "there" yet and live into the unfolding and radical realization that we are always already "here." For it is only "here" that we can really be, wholly present and fully engaged; and no matter where you go, there you are.

PRESENCE ENGAGED

If any want to become followers of mine, let them deny themselves and daily take up their cross and follow after me. For those intent on saving their lives will lose them, and those who let go their life for my sake will save them. What does it profit them to gain the entire world, only to forfeit themselves?—LUKE 9:23-25

What prevents you from being fully immersed in this moment,
the holy ground of "now"?

Every grace-laden moment,
is primed with possibilities
for anyone who is wide open and ready to receive.

The only limit
to our Maker's abundance
is our limited capacity to receive.

Consider a time when you lost yourself
and fell into fullness—
fully alive, fully connected.

Passion, along with her seasoned sibling, compassion,
astonishment that ripens into awe,
and wonder that blossom into gratefulness

are portals into Presence that penetrates
illusory separateness and leave us
beside ourselves with joy, with amazement, with grief.

But there is a price to pay
for expansive Presence,
a cost for being fully awake and engaged.

Letting go in lament, getting lost in inspiration,
being piqued by possibility, pained by misery,
or drowned in mystery, all demand a tariff.

Presence exacts its coin—
our dearly held desire for self-preoccupation,
and the fantasy of control that presumes to preside over and above.

Mystics, artists, and prophets exemplify
this surrender into solidarity,
letting the self be moved by suffering and inspired by imagining.

True spiritual practice harbors this same intention—
the hand-over of self that places us on a collision-course with grace
and draws us into a deepened state of readiness.

This holy intention
leads to whole, undivided attention,
where we come to know life in its raw fullness!

Such "wide awake-fulness" finds myriad expression
in three dimensions of holiness:
Presence that is poetic, prophetic, and pastoral.

In the paradox of Presence by getting lost we are found and findable,
by letting go we are upheld and hold others,
by losing our grip on the world we are freed to love with abandon.

I came so they may have life and have it abundantly.—JOHN 10:10

Such three-dimensional Presence
offers the fullness of life promised in the Gospel,
abundantly available to all, especially the most sorely
afflicted among us.

Presence is not gifted for personal sanctification.
It is grace offered that we might perceive and share
the whole heart of our Maker.

Poetic, contemplative Presence
entices us to surrender,
to notice and let life come close.

Prophetic, insightful Presence
disturbs us to the core
and refreshes with a vision of restoration.

Pastoral, consoling Presence
moves us to bless brokenness
with compassionate care.

Like facets of a prism, these three dimensions of life—
accessible to hungry, ready souls—splice love's light
and present us with the many hues of every enduring moment.

Our desire opens a trapdoor of understanding,
and we fall through the surface of things,
tumbling down into Presence.

How will you be present
to the suffering-joy of being alive that presents itself to you
who are poet, prophet, and minister of this unfolding sacred
moment?

Chapter One

Of Darkness and Light

City dwellers are generally less familiar with the dark, its graces along with its dangers. Too readily we reach for the switch to light up our world. Yet, too much light also weakens our eyes even as it pollutes our skies and blinds us to infinite cosmic fields sparkling with timeless, humbling wisdom. For darkness and light cohere, and most of the mysterious universe remains dark to us. This includes unseeable dark energy and possibly immeasurable quantities of dark matter.

Darkness is necessary. All life germinates in the dark, and we spend fully one half of our lives in that state. Without pervasive darkness there would be no need for light, and still there are places and realities that light cannot illumine. Lightlessness also bears different aspects. It is the impenetrable cloak of mystery that hides the Holy and shades our lives with the nuance of not-knowing. Such darkness can both isolate and integrate us under its shadow. When plunged into blackness, our first instinct is to reach out for one another. Should we turn our headlights off, linger long enough in unknowing, and let our eyes adjust to the dimness, we might discover that most especially in dark times we are not alone.

In the dark we all stumble, and when we tread a path into the shadowlands of suffering, we walk carefully on holy ground. The enigmatic backdrop for all enlightenment, darkness must be reverenced, and darker times gift us with opportunities to love, cloaked as burdens.

IN DARKNESS BEGINNING

By the tender mercy of our God, the dawn will break over us from above, to enlighten those who sit under the dark shadow of death, and to guide our feet onto the way of peace.—LUKE 1:78-79

Are you ready to welcome the glimmer of new beginnings?

With fresh fires and Christmas lights,
we mark the darkest days of the rolling year
and call to mind how everything and everyone starts in the dark.

Dark days augur alienation and danger,
yet darkness also draws us together,
a time for dimming our lights so we can see the stars.

This sacred season of birth pangs and beginnings
offers time to lovingly look back
over a year of gifts, of losses, and of lessons.

Pained by opportunities missed,
and the many violations of life,
still we give thanks.

With humility we acknowledge
our general failure to imagine
much more compassionate alternatives to life in these times.

2

And when at last we realize
we don't know where to go,
we are ready to be led into brighter days.

Disciples of the Prince of Peace
live in tension between grief for all that's lost and never can be,
and gratitude for all that's given, an overflow of possibility.

We live in the fullness of time. Every moment is God's own good
time...—THOMAS MERTON

May the darker seasons invite you to dream and scheme,
starting with gratitude, softened by repentance,
and ignited with longing for restoration.

An ancient blessing renewed
for all who are heart-sore,
worried, or wondering at this time of turning:

Deep Peace of the running wave, and the cleansing of the waters.
Deep Peace of the flowing air, and the clearing of the skies.
Deep Peace of the soft rain, and the shelter of friendship.
Deep Peace of shining stars, and the memory of timeless beginnings.
Deep Peace of the quiet earth, and the kinship of all creatures.
Deep Peace of the gentle night, and the warm hearth of family.
Deep Peace of the ancient stones, and the tenacity of life.
Deep Peace of the heart of Mary, and the tender touch of every
mother.
Deep Peace of the Christ child, and the Holy One guised as enemy
and kin.

Deep Peace of our merciful Maker, and the Spirit who makes us one. To the terrors of the night, and the troubles of your day, Deep Peace.—CELTIC TRADITIONAL, ADAPTED

FACING THE DARK

Concerned and agitated, Jesus said to them, "I am saddened so deeply, even to death; remain here and stay awake with me."
—MATTHEW 26:38

What happens when you out-stare the darkness of our days?

When you drive the suburbs at night,
red-eyed nocturnal creatures
reflect the glare.

Travel the labyrinth of any darkened city
and you can spot other night-dwellers,
captivated in momentary flashes.

If you slow down
for a brief visual connection,
you might meet the mirrored look of creatures caught in the high beam;

that gaze found on dazed faces
when picking up the shreds
after violations by forces of nature or terror.

Always, there is more than meets the eye,
more struggle, mystery, hope, pain, joy, and disappointments deep,
all hidden behind faces that pass us by.

I find myself in the primordial
lostness of the night, solitude,
forest, peace, a mind
awake in the dark...
—THOMAS MERTON, "Day of a Stranger"

So much goes on unknown, unseen.
After dark, a society of the night comes to life, often illuminated
momentarily by swirling red and blue strobes, punctuated by siren
screams.

Nightly, we witness deadly danger play out as news.
Before giving ourselves over to sleep, we lock doors against the night,
praying that such shadows might pass us over.

Can we see the traumas, trials, and terrors of the night
with different eyes, through the merciful lens
of the Maker of day and darkness?

As you slide the deadbolt tonight,
let your compline be a nocturnal benediction
on night-dwellers and overnight workers.

HEART-SIGHT

"Here is an astonishing thing! You do not know where he comes
from, and yet he opened my eyes."—JOHN 9:30

Whose eyes do you seek out, whose gaze do you avoid?

There is insight and oversight,
revision and examination;
then there is heart-sight, seeing from within with rinsed eyes.

Some gazes captivate; other looks are withering,
and the clear-eyed charm of children
changes the pallor of everything.

As eyesight dims with age,
it becomes harder to find focus and clarity,
yet this need not result in loss of vision.

The only true voyage of discovery, the only fountain of Eternal
Youth, would be not to visit strange lands but to possess other
eyes. —MARCEL PROUST, *In Search of Lost Time*

Surely the years
will weaken us
with aches and twinges that foretell frailty.

But fading sight, slowing fragility, and inevitable dependency,
also afford us graces
that germinate in the dark.

...there were lovely things in the world, lovely only that didn't
endure, and the lovelier for that... Nothing endures."
—LEWIS GRASSIC GIBBON, *Sunset Song*

And there will be times
when we must face our fear to forgive and be forgiven,
to rage from our core and speak out against injustice.

Nor can we underestimate
how hard it always is
to embody compassion.

For this demands the determination
to walk with others into places
where we are weak, vulnerable, broken together.

First, we must dare to look upon
the wide-open world of woe and fear,
(and most especially our least-loved foes) with eyes rinsed clear.

For every form of blindness
also teaches trust and humble reliance,
reaching out to another for steadiness, redirection, and courage.

Before our eyes, beneath our feet,
at the tips of our noses and fingers,
a universe of possibility lingers.

May the blessing of the rain
beat upon and wash your spirit fair and clean,
leaving a pool where the blue heaven shines,
and sometimes also a star.
—CELTIC BLESSING, ADAPTED

Amid all the disaster and distress
that wheels around and swirls within us in chaotic times,
there are also always marvels to behold.

Let neither fear nor preoccupation
keep you from being touched
by wonderfully wounded life.

May you find a way in every day
to share your great-fullness
for all that touches your eyes.

May you refuse to be crushed,
but rather, look lovingly upon all with tear-washed eyes,
trained on woundedness, straining for wonder.

As you savor the sweet brevity of your days,
may passion puncture you, letting out joy,
till warmly you are welcomed: a sight for sore eyes.

LET IN THE LIGHT

The body's lamp is the eye. So, if your eye is clear, your entire body will be enlightened; but if your eye is cloudy, your whole body will be filled with darkness. Then, if the light within you is darkened, how great will that darkness be!—Matthew 6:22-23

What images have you absorbed today with the daylight?

Looking back to childhood,
I am struck
by how often we had our windows cleaned.

Every other week,
with ladder, bucket, and cloth,
a window-cleaner appeared.

After a wash and wipe,
crystal clarity
brought into sharper focus both beauty and blight.

If the doors of perception were cleansed everything would appear to [us] as it is, infinite.—WILLIAM BLAKE, "The Marriage of Heaven and Hell"

8

With each passing moment
countless images flicker
before our ever-hungry eyes.

Such a volume of visual stimulation
illuminates optic nerves
and fires frenzied neurons in our brains.

Cascading thoughts,
ideas, visions, and sensations
course through our pulsing core.

Picture the graphic noise and images
that illustrate
the news of just one day:

moving messages and retinal flashes,
tinted by culture, colored by ideology,
all refracted through the passion and pain we call perspective.

What today have you seen or selected,
overlooked or filtered,
blindly blocked or deftly deflected?

No eye has ever seen, nor has any ear heard, nor has any human
heart yet conceived, what the Holy One has in store for those who
love God—these things has God revealed to us through the Spirit;
for the Spirit probes everything, even the depths of the Holy
One.—1 CORINTHIANS 2:9-10

Whether clouded by confusion,
fogged by anger, steamed with passion,
smudged by cynicism,

or made dusty with distraction,
the opaque lens of the soul
requires regular wiping.

We can learn to cut through clutter to clarity,
and welcome whatever life presents
with the bright-fresh eyes of a child.

We don't see things as they are. We see things as we are.—TALMUD

If you are about Gospel work,
with a head for justice and a tender heart,
it helps each day to cleanse the lens.

We dare not disregard the darkness,
nor turn away from problems and pain;
but face instead each morning's light and bathe our
eyes in mercy's rain.

When the world looks always grimy,
when hope and newness are obscured,
then is the time for window wiping.

Cleanse the panes with wonder and lament
for the tears of sorrow and laughter you share;
let love's light in to dissipate despair.

No matter where your eyes come to rest,
will you look long enough and lovingly,
till light breaks through at last?

O God, create in me a clean heart,
and deep within place a renewed and a steadfast spirit.
—PSALM 51:10

LIGHT REFLECTED

"As long as I am in this world, I am the light of the world."
—JOHN 9:5

Have you missed the miracle of today, or did it wake you up to wonder?

It's happening right now;
somewhere out there
daylight is dawning.

That fresh gift of morning
has already graced us all, as bleary-eyed
we rolled from shadow into nuclear radiance;

a momentous transmutation
of hydrogen into helium, casting out enormous energy
to shatter the all-surrounding gloom.

Every millisecond of existence,
this sacrificial spectacle
enlightens the frigid immensity of the void.

At 186 thousand miles per second,
solar outbursts hurtle across 93 million miles
to wake us, warm us, make us squint.

And we may blink and blindly say:

"It's just the sun. It happens every day."
After all, it has been reliably radiating for over four billion years.

Yet, if the miracle of sunshine
fails to impress or startle us from our stupor,
perhaps we are simply blinded by the glare.

The only thing worse than being blind is having sight but no vision. —HELEN KELLER

In this world darkened by despair and deep division,
we fumble dimly
to see past self-interest, fears, and endless feuding.

But even looking down we can see beyond,
like the pilgrim seeking clarity
who found a limpid pool,

and bending down glimpsed
the Milky Way
mirrored in the deep.

Then gazing heavenward,
gaped and gasped
at the cosmic show above,

while awe-filled silence taught:
the stiller you become,
the clearer will your reflection be.

Then shall blinded eyes be opened,
and deaf ears unstopped;

12

then shall the lame ones leap like deer,
and speechless voices sing for joy.—ISAIAH 35:5-6

If we are
not yet astonished,
we are not quite awake!

God-willing, we will be blessed by another sunrise
to break open our hearts and bring us to our knees.
But none will exactly be like this shining, singular morning.

So, as our world rolls, dawn to dusk,
we contemplate the countless faces
whose loves and longings sunlight graces.

From the rising of the sun to its setting
the name of the Holy One be praised.—PSALM 113:3

Then each life illumined in morning bright
will reflect that merciful light
to everything under the sun that lands within our sight.

SEEDING HOPE

To what might we compare God's Realm, what parable might
describe it? It is like a mustard seed, which, when cast into the soil,
is the tiniest of all seeds on earth; yet, when sown, grows into the
greatest of all shrubs, sending out branches large enough for the
birds of the air to make their nests in its shade.—MARK 4:30-32

When desperation reigns, where do you turn for hope?

An honest assessment of our times
yields little reason for optimism, but ample grounds for hope
embedded in the humus of our humanity.

When facing disaster
and unable to change the weather,
our only recourse is to sink roots deeper.

Thus, weathering drought, flood or fire,
and undermining the twin despairs of division and indifference,
we might still harbor seeds of hope to sustain us.

O Holy One, come to my assistance, hasten God to help me!
—PSALM 69:2

Intoning this plea
on behalf of the truly desperate
invites a solidarity of soul.

It is so necessary in these times
for us to grow down,
always attentive to the caveat: the deeper—the darker!

If we want to seed hope,
we must first allow our vision
to become accustomed to the dark.

What you sow, you reap...if you sow to the Spirit, life unending you
will reap.—GALATIANS 6:7-8

Among the triumvirate of enduring virtues,

hope is a choice, born of faith that brings love to life.
No hope without faith, no love without hope!

Yet, hope cannot be tended alone.
It is conjured, in dark conspiracy, by two or three or more
who dare invoke the dangerous memory of Jesus.

So, if hope is what you long to see
then first you'll have to find that WE—
at least one bold bunch of two or three.

For only together can we trace
the filaments of hope threading darkly
through the stories of the people we encounter.

Hope is not something to be found outside of us. It lies in the spiritual life we cultivate within.—JOAN CHITTISTER, *Scarred by Trouble, Transformed by Hope*

Christian disciples are curators
of the delicate seedlings of hopefulness,
hiding in the hungry eyes of God's children.

So, look lovingly around
and see the hopeful glimmer
in newborn eyes, fresh and fearless.

Hope is definitely not the same thing as optimism. It is not the conviction that something will turn out well, but the certainty that something makes sense, regardless of how it turns out.
—VÁCLAV HAVEL, *Disturbing the Peace*

May you take care to tend to each other,
and turning your face to the sun,
let the shadows fall behind you.

CHANGEABILITY

The wind blows where it will, and you hear its sound,
but you know not from whence it came or whence it's bound.
So it is with all, of the Spirit born.—JOHN 3:8

What might you do to change this world?

When the climate changes—
whether political or environmental—
as it is wont to do,

and we are powerless to affect it,
we can
sink our roots deeper;

deeper than fire and flood;
deeper than drought and despair;
deeper than fear and fury;

beyond and below the reach
of trends, tempests, and
even traumas.

When the wind shifts—
whether social, cultural, or religious—
as it is prone to do,

and we cannot redirect it,
we can
reset our sails.

In prayerful attention
we sink our souls deeper
to ground ourselves in the Perennial Presence.

In prophetic contemplation
we raise our sails
into the Prevailing Power,

to harness the momentum
that inspires
the restless turn of time and tide.

So, rather than run
we can also choose
to root our souls.

And rather than attack
the blow and bluster,
we can also learn to tack into it.

Thus, do we chart a course,
aligned with
the cosmic sweep of stars,

and pattern our lives,
attuned to that radiant, perpetual pulse;
the Sacred Hub of Compassion.

and remember
blessings
within brokenness,
beginnings
within endings,
and beauty
within all things.
—BERNADETTE MILLER, *A Serious Frivolity*

In a universe in constant motion,
change is always coming,
the revolving refrain of a grand celestial dance.

Through this ceaseless movement of wind and weather
in world affairs, one question remains:
How will we receive, respond to, and reflect changeability?

We have already entered
the rough waters and rapids of global climate change,
with all its incumbent social upheaval.

Yet, our ancestors also endured trials,
weathering the turbulence of conquests, empires,
and global wars that bred ethnocide and genocide.

Now, we face the fearful possibility of ecocide—
the mindless despoilment of the one home, loaned by our Maker
for those living generations yet to come.

And perhaps never before in history's long arc
has the inheritance of so many
been squandered so swiftly by the recklessness of so few.

For change is surely upon us, and changes are sorely needed.

Each alone, and all together,
we must weigh the price of change with the cost of inaction,

so that, rooted deeply and reaching widely,
we might remain anchored through the shifting seasons
as we navigate the tumultuous currents of our treacherous times.

And may you, dear seeker,
care enough to bare your soul
and daringly raise a sail that will lead us to a change of course.

Chapter Two

Of Love and Loss

Should you look for consolation without cost,
fulfillment without loss,
and wisdom without letting go,
deep delusion shall you meet, tightly wrapped as woe.

Unlike our ancestors, we live privileged lives, enjoying more comforts and opportunities than the ancients could ever have imagined. Yet none of us is immune to suffering, nor can we afford to remain oblivious to the costs, borne by the earth and her impoverished people, of the violations that result from highly consumptive living.

Here is the seed that must be cracked for us to grow: The narrow doorway into fuller, deeper living is called suffering, which can be another name for love. And, while suffering can ennoble as it humbles, so much of it is needless while all the rest is necessary. But none of it should be romanticized or spiritualized. For suffering-love bears the hardest, most fruitful harvest in anyone's life. Passion is the hard part of compassion, the shadow cast by the light of love. A shadow wherein the hidden Holy One awaits.

Yet the perennially persistent questions still resound: Why must we suffer? Why does loving hurt so? Why so much pain in living? Like a crying infant, suffering will not be ignored. There is grace in loss, loving, and letting go, but it is dark grace; it hides in our unknowing; it awaits us in our uncertainty; it is eager for our indignation at pain; it calls out of us a trusting response we have named faith.

In the latticework of the universe, what gossamer strands hold it all together?

Is it love? Is it pain? And, is suffering shared simply the shadow side of love?

Touch one thread and all the rest trembles.

LOVE HURTS

This is my command, that you love each other as I have loved you. No one can have greater love than this, to lay down your life for your friends.—JOHN 15:12-13

When have you loved painfully?

There are places
on our precious planet
that never fail to move me.

There are people in my life
I like and admire,
who always seem to inspire.

There are tastes,
sights, sounds, activities
that give me joy.

I might say "I love"
these places, people,
things to see and do.

What I mean is;
they bring pleasure, even joy, and
fill my days with delight; they are good gifts.

Beloved, let us love one another, because love is from God;
everyone who loves is born of God and knows God. Whoever does
not love does not know God, for God is love. —1 JOHN 4:7-8

There are also places
I avoid, people I fear
and deeply dislike.

There are realities
in our world I despise,
differences, difficulties, I cannot reconcile.

There are transgressions
in my life that are shameful,
experiences I am unable to accept, abhorrent actions and attitudes.

Try as I might,
I cannot escape
these distressing aspects of life.

Yet, there is another, disturbing dimension,
a level of connection, a place of encounter,
embrace and engagement.

This state of being,
beyond like or dislike,
defies adequate description.

It lacks those hardened boundaries
that keep reality at arm's length:
objective, separate, manageable.

What we call "love"
is so often misrepresented,
so broadly misunderstood.

Here is a costly truth,
learned by letting love take me out of bounds,
across lines of affection and disaffection: Love hurts!

This does not mean we allow
people to abuse or exploit us or anyone.
Suffering-love neither quails nor quivers!

It boldly demands that we listen,
let life look us in the eye,
and see our true selves mirrored in our care.

Suffering-love dismantles barricades. Where there is a barrier—
"*This far shall I love and no further!*"— we remain within the limits of
affection, protecting ourselves from love's harshest truth.

Suffering-love is a liberating force.
It neither clings nor holds captive.
It is expressed only in raw release.

Everyone, everything we love, we must let go.
We know how deeply we love—something, someone, our lives—
in that wrenching act of letting go.

The deeper the love,
the more devastating
the letting go.

Love all God's creation, the whole and every grain of sand of it.
Love every leaf, every ray of God's light. Love the animals, love
the plants, love everything. If you love everything, you will
perceive the divine mystery in things.—FYODOR DOSTOYEVSKI,
The Brothers Karamazov

At this poignant-painful point
of relinquishment,
we enter the blissful-broken heart of our Greatest Lover:

the Most Moved Mover,
whose essence is life-giving,
liberating, suffering-love.

Now at last can we know
how the Holy One feels.
May it be so for you.

There is no fear in love, but perfect love casts out fear.—1 JOHN 4:18

IN LOVE'S SHADOW

When Jesus saw her weeping, and those with her also weeping, he
was disturbed to the core and deeply moved. He said, "Where have
you laid him?" They said to him, "Master, come and see." Jesus
started to sob. So they said, "See how much he loved him!"
—JOHN 11:33–36

How has loving pained you?

Despite popular mythology,
our lives are not seasoned by achievement or adulation.
They are sorely stretched by loving, losing, and letting go.

Aching for intimate connection
and the solace and sweetness of mutual affection,
willingly we overlook the sting of suffering that cuts cruelly in love's
wake.

And suffering is such rude awakening.
Whether pained directly or absorbing the hurt of those in our care,
we writhe and wrestle with our impenetrable shadow.

No spirituality can be of lasting value or provide adequate nourishment which has not faced the realities of despair and dereliction.—
KENNETH LEECH, *Experiencing God*

Loving a friend, partner, parent, sister, or brother,
inevitably invites us
to walk the halls of this most sorrowful mystery.

Who does not dread the late-night call,
the rush to a hospital bed, the release of that last, sweet breath,
or the lifeless remnant of our beloved?

If love is letting go,
then in that final moment when we let our dear one depart,
at last we come to know what it is to really love.

Rubbed raw,

such losses leave us exposed, chafed raw,

and sensitive to every pain in the world.

Why so much soreness,

such hunger for connection in the midst of alienation?

Why must birthing, growing, loving, living, ageing, dying...hurt us so?

Founded on doubts and questions,

faith is not a fix for overcoming obstacles.

It is for experiencing them, all the way through.

And there is sharp honesty in suffering.

Bereft of adequate answers, we weep for all that is lost

and cross a threshold into another country: a different kind of

solidarity.

Though I traverse the vale of death's dark shadow,
I fear no evil, for you are with me...—PSALM 23:4

Could such suffering be love's shadow,

and might loss be the necessary corridor to lament—

the liberation of letting go?

No joy without sorrow, no love without grief.

The deeper the joy, the wider the love,

the more space for suffering to inhabit.

At home, each room holds a crucifix

announcing "God-hanging-with-us" in torment:

the embodiment of love in its cruel, contorted awe-fullness.

So close in our darkness, so linked to our loss
is this long-languishing Christ,
that we can mistake passionate intimacy for absence.

If the Holy One is love, and love keenly cuts,
then, pained in loving, finally we come to know
what our Most Holy Lover feels like.

God is love, and any who abide in love abide in God, and God
abides in them.—1 JOHN 4:16

Love's shadow reveals a conduit to all suffering.
Pierced and penetrated by loss,
we dwell in the pall that compassion casts in our world.

No longer do we live
in fear of retribution
or expectation of reward.

And this Realm of Compassion
does not propose a life free from suffering and loss—
read the Beatitudes!

Rather, it reflects that state where pain is transfigured,
where in suffering-shared, we are enlightened
by our closeness with the hurting-healing Holy Presence.

So, when we enter sorrow's shade,
we are stirred by the heartbroken cry of our Maker,
echoed in the shattered lives scattered around about us.

PASSION REVISITED

Remain in me as I remain in you.—JOHN 15:4

How does the Passion touch you?

As young ones take to the streets for their lives
amid the terror of our time,
Christ suffers still with each unjust, atrocious crime.

Despised and rejected, full of suffering,
acquainted with infirmity;
someone from whom others hid their faces,
whom we held of no account.—ISAIAH 53:3

It was early in the spring,
some years back—
before he became yet another homicide victim—

that a longtime neighbor from the streets
came looking for consolation
amid the torment of his days.

As always, the disturbing,
persistent door chime
guaranteed a most inconvenient intrusion.

Let this darkness be a bell tower
and you the bell. As you ring,
what batters you becomes your strength.
—RAINER MARIA RILKE, *Sonnets to Orpheus II*

Peering through the fisheye,
I recoiled at that gaunt, familiar face
blankly staring back.

Yet, just before he moved to leave,
reluctantly, I turned the handle,
that opened my life to his.

Wracked and reduced by cancer,
painfully distorted, he managed an impish smile,
as unabashed, once more he came begging:

for the shattered soul, a hearing;
for the weary world, some wrinkled notes;
for the broken body, a piece of fruit.

All repaid in full, with a bony hug,
and a prescient request: *"Will you be my pall bearer?"*
Then, one last, whispered intimation: *"You know I love you!"*

Children let us love not merely in word or speech, but in deed and
in truth.—1 JOHN 3:18

From the window,
I watched his lumbered,
hobbling departure.

Holding up pants
long ago too large for a wasted body,
he waved behind him.

At full voice, he cried
his thanks to the wind,
daring the neighbors to ignore him.

Since my people are crushed, I AM crushed;
I mourn, and horror seizes me.
Is there no balm in Gilead?
Is there no physician there?
Why then is there no healing for the wound of my people?
—JEREMIAH 8:21-22

This Christ presence
has long since hung about me.
Still today, I can perceive his scent and song.

In peripheral vision and rearview mirrors,
I glimpse his reflection flashed
in eyes and faces unknown.

As for me,
I can no longer uncover that boundary
which marks the separation between him and me, and the Holy
Other.

It seems to [the soul] that the entire universe is a sea of love in
which it is engulfed, for, conscious of the living point or center of
love within itself, it is unable to catch sight of the boundaries of
this love.—JOHN OF THE CROSS, *The Living Flame of Love*

As you plumb the mysteries
of dying to live
in days and weeks most holy,

may the blessed-broken Christ
come close enough to contaminate you
with the contagion of compassionate care.

What shape might compassion take in your life?

DYING TO LIVE

Why search for the living among the dead? He is not here but has
risen. —Luke 24:5

How do you embrace the living and dying within the reach of your arms?

In a Rwandan marketplace,
I picked up a carved, Y-shaped twig
in the likeness of a person with arms outstretched.

Captivated by this Christ image,
I questioned the craftsman:
"Is this Christ crucified or risen?"

With a beaming smile,
the vendor responded,
"Both!"

Like every other
encounter in Rwanda,
this response provoked newness out of me.

But first, I protested.
*"How can this be? Surely, it's one or the other;
either dying and dead or risen and living."*

Flashing another brilliant smile,
he shook a calloused finger;
"In Rwanda, Christ is always dancing between dying and living."

Either the world is coming together
or else the world is falling apart ...
—PETER COLE, "Song of the Shattering Vessels"

With increasing frequency,
losses, letting go, and dying
come tightly wrapped into living.

Each time I let myself be moved
by the aches of neighbors dear and distant,
I am drawn down into the broken, Sacred Heart.

So strange,
how I have also savored joy
in these tender, touching encounters.

When I wait for life to come into focus,
or lean into the news of the day,
I perceive the strains of this dying-rising dance.

Like buds on blackened branches,
or that hint of rotting fruit
in the scent of the blossom,

joy and suffering, darkness and illumination,
living and dying emerge and subside;
fluid movements in a seamless symphony.

When we welcome life's changing seasons gracefully,
arms flung wide,
we affirm our faith in darkness before birth;

in life before death; in love leading to the cross;
in the cross opening a doorway to unimagined breadth of being
—compassionately contorted and connected.

All that is asked
is a willingness to bear witness
and abide in the belly of paradox;

to place ourselves in between the poles,
to straddle inner and outer conflicts,
to deny categories and to defy divisiveness.

Resurrection beckons
whenever we make space for the needs,
deficiencies, and potential of our fellow pilgrims.

Hung between opposing forces,
the cruciform Christ
illustrates the power of dying to live:

eternal icon to the mystery
that dying also makes room
for something new and unforeseen.

If we can but die to our need to be right,
might we also crack open a space
wide enough

to hold the impact of our global consumptive culture;

to lament social deprivation and planetary desecration;
to begin together to undo ethnic, national, religious supremacies?

Surely these "dyings"
connect us to holy,
humble, hurting, and healing lives.

Come life-giving Spirit most wholly;
lead us in your birling dance,
from death to birth and back again!

LOVE IS LISTENING

I am the voice of someone who cries out in the wilderness, "Make
the way of the Holy One straight." —JOHN 1:23

Who in your world cries out for your attention?

If listening is what lovers do,
our Maker is all ears,
attuned to every creature's cry that voices hopes and fears.

Authentic prayer abandons words,
with nothing else to do,
except unwrap its golden gift—a hearty listening to.

Contact with people who are crying out... is one of the most
important nourishments in our lives. —JEAN VANIER,
Community and Growth

Listen and *silent* are anagrams,
and any quiet listener
will soon be shown who and how to love.

The first and final sound we speak
is the breathy gasp that draws us in,
and the sigh that carries us out.

Have you followed the music
of your lungs this day,
or attended the breathing of your neighbors?

We do not simply catch our breath;
we gratefully receive and graciously return it,
for this is the calculus of contemplation.

Choosing to stop and listen,
with hearts attentive and attuned,
is the first brave step toward true encounter.

Listen! At the door I stand knocking; if you hear my voice and open
the door, I will enter and eat with you and you with me.
—REVELATION 3:20

Deeper listening
extends a wide welcome,
hospitality to heal and make us whole.

Open-hearted hearing weaves us
into one another's stories,
implicating and entangling us in larger lives.

Listening with soul
demands deliberate presence and dedicated availability,
a willingness to drop the protections of privilege.

Blessed are the listeners who tread
the sacred soil of other lives
and bare their soles to bear silent witness.

Then Mary replied, "Behold the handmaiden of the Holy One; let it
be with me according to your word."—LUKE 1:38

In days like these,
who pays attention
to humble aspirations?

And who cares to heed
the voices of women
and girls?

Yet redemption rests
entirely on the response of
such faithful, fearless voices.

When a blessed peasant girl
declared her consent,
the messenger of mercy took heed, while all creation gasped.

Let anyone who has ears to hear listen!—MARK 4:9

Listening likens us to our Maker
and makes of us messengers of gladness
who declare to the wilderness of our times...

To everything and everyone...Love listens
With careful attention...Love listens
For the little people and the lost...Love listens

To hopes, hurts, and hungers...Love listens
To the cry of the earth
and the cry of the poor...Love listens

To fears, failings, shame, and sorrow...Love listens
To regrets and rejections...Love listens
To a world of pain and possibility...Love listens

This poor soul cried out, was listened to by the Holy Hearer, and was saved from every trouble.—PSALM 34:6

May you cultivate a hearing heart,
ever ready to receive and
always eager to return forgiveness.

And may we all take to heart
and breathe this truth:
Love is listening!

MIND THE GAP!

How often have I desired to gather your children together as a mother hen gathers her brood under her wings, and you were not willing.—LUKE 13:34

Can we bear witness to a gospel that gathers together in a world bent on tearing apart?

On stations with curved platforms,
London Underground passengers are familiar
with an electronic voice that warns: '*Mind the gap!*'

In days like these,

we might direct that same mindful alert

to the widening crevasse that would cleave reality into duality.

Where is the healing vision of wholeness

amid all the siding and separating

that dissects each expression of "us" into opposing camps?

It might help to be mindful of the gaps

when we feel the draw to divide lives and love

into contradictory categories:

weeds over wheat; enemy over friend;

rich over poor; left over right;

black over white; faith over science;

love of God over neighbor love;

grace over works; action over contemplation;

wisdom over information; people over creation.

What would happen to our seeing

thinking, acting, and understanding,

if we were to convert our conjunctions,

turning *over* into *and*,

letting *and*

become *with*?

"Master, did you not sow good seed in your field? Then where did
these weeds come from?" "An enemy has done this," he answered.
The servants said, "Then do you want us to go and gather them?"
But he replied, "No; by gathering the weeds you would uproot the

wheat along with them. Let them both grow together until the
harvest."—MATTHEW 13:27-30

A genocide memorial in Rwanda tells of high-school girls,
directed at gunpoint to divide into tribal groups.
Instead, they linked arms and declared: *"We refuse to be separated!"*

As we denounce divisiveness, and the normalizing of hatred,
we can also expose the fear behind it
by claiming our fundamental communion.

Oppositional dichotomies
only reduce us all to caricatures
that fail to respect the mystery and complexity of every life situation.

Though distinctions and divisions are very real
and really important,
life thrives only in diversity.

And when this interwoven fabric is threatened,
we must declare that torn apart we cannot grow,
for we can only grow together.

Without complementarity, how can we be complete?
So, when our circle of care contracts,
or we spiral into divisiveness, we cry out:

Spirit of Oneness
heal and make us whole!
Help us mend the gap between:
   who we are and how we live;
   those we call friend and those who call us enemy;
   heads and hearts;

between…

    yearning for peace and quiet;

    and longing for peace with justice;

    craving for meaning and hungering for food;

between…

    policies and practices;

    good intentions

    and available resources;

between…

    words and witness;

    love for God and care for neighbor;

    aspirations and broken relationships.

This unifying mission is far from easy:

to stand in the gap and point the way

from diatribe to dialogue, and from congregation to communion.

BLESSED SACRAMENT OF THE OTHER

When was it we saw you hungry and gave you something to eat, or thirsty and gave you something to drink? And when was it we saw you a stranger and welcomed you, or naked and gave you something to wear? And when was it we saw you sick or in prison and went to visit with you?—MATTHEW 25:37-39

Who would you alienate, cast out beyond the sweep of your concern?

Made to make connections—

thee and *me* becoming WE—

all of us yearn for unanimity.

Craving companionship,
we need to feel part of,
and are afraid of being torn apart from, our common union.

The quality
of our humanity
is calibrated by the breadth of this connectivity.

For none can find wholeness
when the threads of correlation
are systematically severed.

Otherwise, we claim our place in the seamless tapestry,
along with every other creature
lovingly embroidered into a garment called holiness.

Though it wreaks devastation—
torture unspeakable for such profoundly relational beings—
pervasive alienation remains: the Sin of a sundered world.

When the layers of connective tissue
that link us are tattered,
Christ suffers torments unbearable—in minds and bodies shattered.

Isolation haunts homes, hallways, and highways,
wherever we settle for hollow commodity—
a cheap substitute for much more costly community.

Meanwhile, hanging around every corner,
Corpus Christi languishes;
denuded of dignity, devoid of friendship, fettered and famished.

> The Holy One draws near to the heart-broken,
> saving those crushed in spirit. —PSALM 34:18

But mercy tolerates neither exclusion nor exception.
Such exemptions lead only to
dominations and desecrations.

The expanding glow of compassion permits no dark corners,
and no life lies beyond
its warm, infinite, radiant range.

For we are already woven into every other life.
It is the same breath we all share,
free-gifted from forest and fresh ocean air.

We find belonging when we are blessed and broken together.
In such communion we really can taste, touch, see, meet
Christ Presence, in the sacrament of one another.

Connection and care
unlock the tabernacle,
to expose the sacrament most blessed.

The scope of our love is not measured
merely by those we welcome,
but also by those from whom our care is willfully withheld.

> Most truly I tell you, just as you did it to one of the least of these,
> who are members of my family, you did it to me. —MATTHEW 25:40

May you become a daily communicant,
ready to reach out and receive that other sacrament most blest—
Christ-present in every sister and brother.

Chapter Three

Of Simplicity and Slowing

If there's a pearl you cannot hold,
but washes up on wisdom's shore;
it is this teaching, pure as gold—
the key to joy is less is more.

Physics teach that with speed and pressure comes heat and friction, with stress and tension close behind. The antidote to compulsive-comparative living lies in a wholesome embrace of our natural sanctity, the gift of being simply (not super) human. Embracing our imperfect nature gives us permission to forgive and be forgiven, since all of us are made for mercy.

Unpossessed by possessions, we are free to welcome our own poverty of spirit, for only those who know they are incomplete can be made whole. Thus, people who live with less (whether by choice or circumstance) are more likely, in lean times, to lean on Providence and rely on one another. Reverencing our limits lets us share an abundance of simple pleasures and taste the joys of a less-complicated life.

Fast-paced, consumer culture purports to cram our days with stuff and activities, promising to fill the sinkhole at the heart of us with purpose and happiness. Paradoxically, true "holey-ness" widens the ache within, reducing needs, minimizing wants, and clearing the clutter to make room for others. Though a simpler life is intentionally uncomplicated, simple is never easy. It exposes the emptiness of over-filled lifestyles as it celebrates the satisfaction of spacious fulfillment. Simpler also presumes slower. When life reaches that harried and hurried frenetic pitch, it is time for sabbath-slowing, to the pace of God's good time.

Slowing to become available to those who cross our path.
Slowing to match the gait of frailty, the small steps of the aged and toddling infants.
Slowing to pay attention to the contours of life.
Slowing to feel the road beneath our feet.
Slowing to be redirected by a world of need, to learn about loss and longing.

FROM HEAD TO HEART

Blessed are the pure-hearted, for they will see God (in every-thing).—MATTHEW 5:8

Who helps clear a path out of your head and into the heart of our world?

Most of us
come into this world
head first,

the heart following the brain,
till at last
the feet emerge.

Our lifelong journey
toward wholeness
mirrors this top-down trajectory.

They say the head can be fooled but the heart can't turn without
the body.—MARK NEPO, "For Joel at 94"

It starts in the head,
as we rake this world with reason,
desperate to be right, needing to be rewarded,

till those days when
wisdom, wounds, and weariness
muddle the mind with mystery.

Impenetrable graces,
masked as wonder or woe,
push the center deeper down.

Move from within. Don't move the way fear wants you to.
—JALĀL AD-DĪN RŪMĪ

Shedding the fear of being wrong (or punished),
unreasonable love takes the tiller
and, for a time, the heart holds sway.

The lures of love
and the magnetic draw of passion
pull us into one another (and out to every other).

Turned inside out,
we quiver with joyful exhilaration
and shiver at the severities of despair.

Rich in perspective, experienced in failure, the person advanced
in years is capable of shedding prejudices and the fever of vested
interests.—ABRAHAM HESCHEL, *The Insecurity of Freedom*

Now exposed to losses
that shatter the soul,
sweet dreams sour in collision with reality.

Unbidden suffering emerges,
as love's long shadow
casts our whole life in its shade.

Pains, violations, and desecrations on every corner,
enough to take the heart away,
tear at the ragged fringes of our lives.

If failure is life's ballast, at last, we can make a friend of it;
let it steady us while we step deeper
into the mire of holy humanity.

Walking, now with measured step,
in company with the low and slow,
we marinate in the wisdom of love-as-letting-go.

Finally, the feet can take us—
head and heart, body and soul—
where we had always feared to wander.

Without mysticism politics soon become cruel and barbaric;
without political love mysticism becomes sentimental and uncom-
mitted interiority.—EDWARD SCHILLEBEECKX, *On Christian Faith*

Moored in muddiness, wrinkled by worry,
and crinkled with laughter, we release absolutes
as we make our tear-stained truce with ambiguity.

Liberated from the tyrannies
of reason and fickle feelings,
barefoot, we walk this world.

Less sure, but surely more tender,
wonder, gratefulness, and simple pleasures
come back to visit.

Justice, peace, compassion, and sacred wisdom,
deeper than ideas, wider than feelings,
are now embedded in our daily dealings.

Let me seek, then, the gift of silence, and poverty, and solitude,
where everything I touch is turned into prayer: where the sky is my
prayer, the birds are my prayer, the wind in the trees is my prayer,
for God is all in all.—THOMAS MERTON, *Thoughts in Solitude*

May you embrace silence of mind,
solitude of heart, slowness of step
that you might humbly walk in company with the frail and forgotten.

THE GIFT OF FRAILTY

As his fame spread across the country, they brought to him all the
infirm; people afflicted with various diseases and pains; demo-
niacs, epileptics, and paralytics; and he healed all of them.
—MATTHEW 4:24

What have you learned from frailty?

The difference between
a gift and a burden
can be defined by how we receive it.

After major surgery,
I hold a cherished memory
of being feeble, vulnerable, and fearful.

While everyone around me moved with ease,
I needed to be steadied
and patiently accompanied.

An inner tutor whispered:
"Hold onto this perspective. Welcome this gift of fragility.
Do not be too eager for the world of the self-reliant."

Strengthen hands that are feeble, make firm knees that are weak,
say to frightened hearts:
Be strong, fear not! Here comes your God.—ISAIAH 35:3

Still there are places
where obviously broken people
are discounted as "in-valid."

But wisdom welcomes weakness,
whether physical, moral, or emotional,
as life's greatest teacher.

Learning from limitation and debilitation
lets us lean on one another,
and therein know a humble-healing communion of care.

These are surely costly lessons to bear,
for we dare not sugar-coat
the pain and sorrow that come with living.

Yet these darker graces of suffering
teach dear lessons about the cost of loving,
the pain of growing, the anguish of letting go.

Infirmity can also be a sacred time,
when weathered beauty illuminates dignity
and inspires honesty.

I am struck by how sharing our weakness and difficulties is more
nourishing to others than sharing our qualities and successes.—
JEAN VANIER, *Community and Growth*

Suffering schools us,
and none can grow without stretching and tearing,
losing, and leaving something or someone behind.

There are experiences, relationships, and encounters
that mark us
and leave us forever changed.

And there is no deeper love
than sharing in the sorrow or suffering of another,
a father or mother, a friend or enemy, a sister or brother.

Healing is always a lifelong journey,
integrating the limits and conditions
that are gifted by growth, by illness, and by aging.

By love, pain becomes healing.—JALĀL AD-DĪN RŪMĪ

We need not go looking for frailty,
for no one escapes this life without
some familiarity with suffering and infirmity.

This uninvited teacher can also become a friend,
offering full-body communion with tenuous life
that suffers to give birth, to grow up and down, to love and let go.

Here then is passion—grace that burns
in the solidarity of suffering-shared—
that broken body of Christ, scarred with love's losses and torments.

We are in every way afflicted, but not crushed; perplexed, but not
driven to despair; persecuted, but not forsaken; struck down, but
not destroyed; always carrying in our body the death of Jesus, so
that the life of Jesus might also be made visible in our bodies.
—2 CORINTHIANS 4:8-10

So, when next frailty comes to visit, as surely it will,
may it connect you to the suffering-love of neighbor,
of nature, and of our hurt and healing Maker.

LIVE SMALL

As he was setting out on a journey, a person ran up to him, knelt
before him and asked, "Good Teacher, what should I do in order to
inherit life unending?"—MARK 10:17

What would it cost you to live a little more simply?

Change!
Change!
I need your change!

From the recessed doorway
a voice cries out
to the bustling any-town street.

Shapes of purpose-full people
blur by—
unheeding, unseeing, unaware.

You will surely listen, but never understand, and you will indeed
look, but never perceive. For these people's hearts have become
coarse, their ears are hard of hearing, and they have shut their
eyes.—MATTHEW 13:14

Change!
Change!
I need your change!

Captivated by the call,
a youngster, open-hearted,
turns herself around.

With bright-eyed encouragement,
she addresses the bundled body
that cradles a crinkled cup.

"Don't despair,
change is coming!
We are working for change!"

"I need your change!"
the voice persists
with urgency.

Blushing,
the kind student leans in.
"I'm sorry...you must be hungry!"

Thrusting a handful of coins
into the cup, she adds,
"Perhaps a sandwich, or another cup of coffee?"

To her great surprise,
the hooded head
slowly shakes in disappointment.

"No...
I need YOU
to change your life!"

And what does the Holy One require of you but to do justice, and to love kindness...—MICAH 6:8

Rightly it all begins
with being just—
the pathway to the repair of relationships.

Looking, listening, asking,
with a ready willingness
to be turned around.

This world redeemed
ever needs to be reorganized
by loving-with-sleeves-rolled-up.

Such feeding, healing, forgiving
Gospel work
is only realized in kindness.

For justice
sees and celebrates
our kin in each and anything.

First, be just! Next, be kind!
But then we must change
so much more than just our mind.

...and humbly walk with your God?—MICAH 6:8

For sure,
that third invitation
is the hardest turn of all.

I began to discover that a true spiritual homecoming means a return to the poor in spirit to whom the Kingdom of Heaven belongs.—HENRI NOUWEN, *Seeking Peace*

Live humbly,
simply, slowly!
Keep company with the lowly!

Declarations like these
we seldom see
engraved on marble monuments.

Though it might sound straightforward,
such radical redirection
does not come easily at all.

When true simplicity is gain'd,
To bow and to bend we shan't be asham'd,
To turn, turn will be our delight,
Till by turning, turning we come 'round right.
—TRADITIONAL SHAKER HYMN

May you
content yourself with little.
May you choose a less complicated life.

Share freely
all life's blessings,
and you shall taste well-being.

Live simply that others might simply live!
—ATTRIBUTED TO ELIZABETH ANN SETON

And may we all learn to live small,
because large living is costing the earth—
a price paid most dearly by the littlest lives of all.

SIMPLY FRUGAL

So, stop worrying and asking, "What are we going to eat?" or
"What's to drink?" or "What can we wear?" For it is the faithless
who focus only on these kinds of things.—MATTHEW 6:31-32

Can we just consume less and contemplate more?

Whether by choice or necessity,
only those who live with less
hold thrift in high regard, the expression of a life that is blest.

We do not hear much
about the wisdom of living frugally,
except along the pinched peripheries of society.

The propagation of mass-consumption
conflates being frugal with being miserly
and confuses thrift with meanness of spirit.

Such distortions by market forces are not accidental.
Consider the havoc simple living might wreak on systems
reliant on ever-increasing cycles of mass production and mass
consumption.

Many people know that our current progress and the mere
amassing of things and pleasures are not enough to give meaning
and joy to the human heart, yet they feel unable to give up what the
market sets before them. —POPE FRANCIS, *Laudato Si'*

Now, just imagine, if you can:

enough replacing more;
choosing smaller over bigger;
older over newer; reuse over refuse;

repairing rather than replacing;
home growing and home making over buying and selling;
sharing meals, devices, bicycles, cars;

rejecting built-in obsolescence;
declining upgrades simply to make do;
denouncing dissatisfaction in favor of modest contentment.

Imagine how choosing to reduce, reuse, and rely on others
might herald the demise of predatory commercialism
and derail those deftly marketed illusions, ever on sale.

Frugality presents a radically simple reorientation
that rebuffs "throw-away" living and disposable lives
to redefine "growth" and recast "wealth."

In pursuit of universal well-being,
authentic spirituality becomes a binding force, moving us
below and beyond the reach of restless, acquisitive appetites.

All sins are attempts to fill voids.

—SIMONE WEIL, *Gravity and Grace*

Too accustomed are we to commodities that come at great cost
to the magnificence of earth and her majestic life-forms,
to weary workers, to our own well-being, and to generations to come.

Simply being mindful and careful
helps dispel the enchantments
cast by viral propaganda.

Consider the industry and resources
involved in the creation of the
particular words you are reading.

Reflect on the woodlands, chemicals and fuels,
(processed and refined) necessary to put this poem together.
Call to mind the hands that boxed and shipped and brought this
volume to you.

Consider your car, your shoes, your house,
the energy that lights, heats, and cools your home:
a multitude of touches, countless impacts, and connections taken for
granted.

When expectations are modest,
thrift becomes a common-sense cultivation,
even in times of plenty.

When it comes to simplicity, less is more and less is never easy.
Imagine how these simple invitations
might shape our lives more or less:

walk more, ride less; listen more, talk less;
hold hands more, withhold less;
speak more from the heart, less from the head;

ask forgiveness more readily, hold onto hurt less;
wonder more, worry less;
give more, take less.

How blessed you who are poor in spirit, God's Reign is yours (for
the sharing).—MATTHEW 5:3

Awake to the gifts and costs of living,
we strive to make do with what we have been given
and make sure it goes around.

So, humbly we can walk, sharing more and paring down.
For we are all Godchildren:
thanks-givers, not consumers.

... since we are in your giving image: make us giving like you.
—WALTER BRUGGEMANN, "We Are Takers"

May we be the trusty-thrifty stewards of gifts
for the sharing; the survival of countless creatures
and the lives of our children's children depend upon it.

WONDER-WRAPPED

Blessed are your eyes, for they see, and your ears, for they hear.
—MATTHEW 13:16

Were you ever so wrapped up in the moment that you forgot yourself?

Consider the tragedy
of possibilities left undiscovered
by a present wrapped in wonder that no one bothers to uncover.

Moment by moment
life begs to be unwrapped,
investigated, savored.

No matter where we go,
the primary portals to such loving-fullness
are wonder and her shadow-sister woe.

And wonder is born
when inside-out
we decide to turn.

We need more stillness, more of a sense of wonder, a feeling for
the mystery of life.—BEN OKRI, *Birds of Heaven*

Absorbed, intent, enraptured,
carried away or caught up,
we can lose our self in any awe-filled, breathless moment.

Held captive
by an open-ended present,
explanations evaporate as questions condense.

The practice of awe,
curbs our appetite for analysis,
to leave us quietly wondering.

If we allow the mystery of the moment,
in all its anguished astonishment,
to wrap around us,

like a child we are humbled,
held speechless and shivering,
before pain too deep, or soundless in the face of joy too wide

---

In the formlessness of night and silence a word then pronounces
itself: Mercy.—THOMAS MERTON, "Day of the Stranger"

Wonder demands curiosity and time.
Astonishment asks only for attention,
and no one can pay attention quickly.

When we open curtained eyes to let in delight,
awe carries us beyond the bounds
of this or that, then or there, us or them.

Every day is the last day
of the world that was,
the first day of a world that is becoming.

For the world as we have known it
is always coming to a new beginning—
thanks be to God!

When you search Me out, you will discover Me; if you seek whole-heartedly, I will let you find Me, says your God. —JEREMIAH 29:13

This unrepeatable day, whenever you can,
will you choose to wonder first before you worry,
and let the child within be set free and carried away?

May the tragedies that present themselves crack your heart.
May the possibilities unwrapped blow your mind.
May the miracles of this moment steal your very breath.

The universe is composed of subjects to be communed with,
not primarily of objects to be used. —THOMAS BERRY, *Evening Thoughts*

Without wonder and awe, how else do we to enter into holy communion?

IN GRATEFULNESS GROWING

Jesus asked, "Were not ten of you made clean? Where are the other nine? Has no one else come back to thank the Most High except this foreigner?" Then Jesus said, "Stand up now, you can go on your way; it is your faith that has made you whole." —LUKE 17:12-19

Do you consider yourself a learner or a knower?

Lowliness offers a healthy-holy perspective.
It lays bare our ignorance, illuminates our frailty,
and makes more room for learning and for mystery.

The Gospels teach that there is greatness
in small things, in modest actions,
and in humble people.

Ruler of the universe, I thank you for hiding these things from wise
and knowledgeable people and revealing them to the little ones.
—MATTHEW 11:25

Respect for life (in every form)
is never quite enough,
for we are made for reverence!

Until we are upheld in awe,
though we may survive,
we may not yet be fully alive.

From astounded, to awed, to grateful;
this is the procession to wholly communion—
the fullness of sacramental living.

You are not here to verify,
Instruct yourself, or inform curiosity
Or carry report. You are here to kneel.
—T.S. ELIOT, "Little Gidding"

Humility unlocks gratitude,
so that grounded in gladness,
we might receive whatever life presents.

So much more than saying thank you,
great-fullness is the expression
of our great-littleness.

To be grateful is to succumb
to a more generous, bountiful Spirit
who inoculates us from profane (flat) living...
with wonder (remedy for boredom);
with awe (antidote to hubris);
with gratefulness (cure for cynicism).

Empty-handed, open-hearted humility
is crucial for a life
overflowing with abundance.

Gratitude generates generosity;
the giveaway of heart, mind, and spirit;
transforming an overfilled into a fulfilled life.

And the key to joy lies right here,
in the welcome embrace of what is given,
rather than being acquisition driven.

While we may manufacture fun,
joy will not be fabricated;
it is gift; pure and simple and free!

Nor can joy be withheld;
it is the fruit of sharing gracefully.
Only great fools forget to be grateful.

It is You we praise, Maker of earth and heaven, of the seas and of
all they contain:
You who grants justice for oppressed people;
who provides bread for hungry lives;
who frees all held in captivity;

who opens the eyes of visionless people;
who raises up the ones who are put down;
who loves the just; who protects outsiders; and who holds up
the vulnerable, the parentless and all those who have lost their
spouse.—PSALM 146:6-9

Will you let generosity
liberate someone or something
you have been holding onto or holding back?

LAST AND LASTING

Come to me, all you weary ones, carrying heavy burdens, and I
will give rest to you. Take up my yoke and learn from me; for I am
gentle and humble-hearted, and you will find rest for your souls.
For easy is my yoke and light is my burden.—MATTHEW 11:28-30

What do you leave behind for those coming after you?

As I grow down—creaking, sighing, groaning—
I find my much-diminished self,
ever-closer to the ground.

Bent a bit,
and increasingly inclined
to question rather than resolution,

I am more at home
with the lyrical than the literal
in any and everything: rhyme without reason.

Truth, that once seemed
to fit so neatly
into my travelling haversack,

seems so much larger,
that I can no longer
get my heart, let alone my arms, around it.

Still, wisdom comes by to visit,
gracing my committed incoherence
with room enough for wonder and woe to cohabit.

As tears flow more readily than reasons,
explanations evade me for the monstrous misery I witness,
swept away in a deluge of compassion.

What to tell my dear, growing-up children
after over half a century of wondering and wandering,
looking back more frequently than ahead?

It sounds so simple and simply too hard
that love is where they came from
and all that keeps us going.

...we will be remembered
in the way others still live, and still live on, in our love.
—DAVID WHYTE, "Everlasting," *The Bell and the Blackbird*

And, with the evaporation of absolutes
in the harsh light of mercy,
judgment and dogma dissolve.

Though I cannot quite put my finger on it,
I think, somewhere I must have surrendered,
lost or let go these last illusions of control.

How frightening to be so free,
lightly burdened,
co-responsible for everything, yet in charge of nothing.

Could this be
the uncharted territory I always sought
while playing in the safe confines of the sandbox?

What now remains—last and lasting—
before the long slumber
envelops for good what stood for me.

Now, daily to marry grateful wonder with grace-filled woe
and find, in that blessed arrangement, stepping-stones
to help in my stumbling toward the wholeness called well-being.

May it be so for you, fellow pilgrim,
as you make your way home,
much more deeply into here, far less concerned with hereafter.

And in your seeking, may you be found
and found out, as a wise fool, whose supple heart,
cleaved by loss and love, may never again close to mercy and mystery.

Now rest and be thankful!

Chapter Four

Of Wholeness and Holiness

Love is little, love is low,
love will make our spirits grow.
Grow in peace, grow in light,
love will do the thing that's right.
—TRADITIONAL SHAKER HYMN

Holiness brings us down to earth and into our wholly human nature to learn and relearn how to be and behave as children of the earth. To be holy is to be connected, rooted in the ground of our being. It means humbly knowing our place, living up to and out of our original blessedness. Holy really means lowly. If only we could embody this wisdom!

We are the lowly-holy earthlings, part of, not apart from, the myriad evocations of life on a miraculous life-making planet. Holy also means wild. For Jesus, too, wandered the wilderness to be with the beasts and be ministered to by the angels. So imbued are we with a transcendent spark of consciousness that we are also fleeting images of our mysterious Source, in whom we all live and move and have our being.

We do not, cannot, make ourselves holy, for we are already inherently sacred. This divine indwelling is not a commodity that can be manufactured, acquired, or won. It is the shimmering mirror of our

Maker, imprinted in the spiraling, double helix DNA of our and every being. It is a gift we cherish and nurture with the daily blessings of sunshine and showers. And blessedness is a gift we cannot keep, but only share, when we live out of our own sanctity by lifting up the sacredness of every other and working to create a whole world that honors holiness universal.

In the midst of much commotion,
blessed because you are broken.
and broken in order to be blessed,
this holy-ness is also our holy mess;
gift of broken openness.

WHOLEHEARTED

You shall love the Holy ONE with your whole heart, your entire soul, the fullness of your mind, and all your strength.
—MARK 12:30

What merits your wholehearted attention these days?

We are living through a time of extremes,
where the so much taken by so few
leaves too little for too many;

where understanding and forbearance
are held hostage
by fanaticism and fear;

where hateful brutality
comes garbed as religion,
and callous cynicism dresses up as freedom.

Yet, it is deeper into this disturbing wasteland
that we are beckoned
to bare our hearts to a plea;

the keening chorus
of tenuous life,
sorely afflicted:

echoed in the churning storms
and crackling glaciers
of warming-wasted oceans,

amid the chafing cries
of God's children cast adrift
on treacherous seas.

Within this refrain lives
the deepest longing
of Our Long-Suffering Lover aching for healing.

May you know the urgency with which God longs for you.

—JOHN O' DONOHUE, "For Longing," *To Bless the Space Between Us*

It begs us to leave hearts ajar
and comforts behind,
that would only harden the crusty edges of our care.

The wilderness of compassion hides seeds,
dry and dormant, anticipating catharsis—
the melting of hearts, the changing of minds and lives.

Wildness reminds us what it means to be human, what we are
connected to rather than what we are separated from.
—TERRY TEMPEST WILLIAMS

These packages of possibility hold blueprints for peace
that blossom with the merest inclination of reverence,
and precipitation of tenderness.

In a world such as this,
who has the courage
to be vulnerable first?

Who dares confront
untruths, terror, and taunting
with the hot truth of tears?

Who is strong enough to be gentle,
willing enough to embody the paradox:
Only the broken are made whole-hearted?

Vulnerability is the only reliable measure of courage.
—BRENÉ BROWN

Though in her manifold dimensions
universe looks like chaos,
at her core mysterious, she is profound connection,

light itself, ever-outreaching,
craving communion—deep calling out to deep
in a singular cosmic sacrament!

Will you quiet your soul,
steady your voice,
and ready your loved ones for wholehearted living,

so that lovingly we might stand together,
before the haze of hurt and hatred,
misguided mockery, and the reckless ruination of holy life?

It is when we love the most intensely and most humanly that
we can recognize how tepid is our love for others. The keenness
and intensity of love brings with it suffering, of course, but joy
too because it is a foretaste of heaven. When you love people,
you see all the good in them, all the Christ in them.
—DOROTHY DAY, *On Pilgrimage*

Will you weep and keenly wonder
at the state of God's good garden
and wounded humanity—body-broken of Christ?

Wholehearted living—compassion practiced—
is a narrow gate into Mercy's expansive realm
that evaporates separation to draw us more tightly together:

the dominated with the divided,
the gated with the segregated, the distracted with the discounted,
the privileged with the persecuted people of God,

together at last
under the beams we all bear,
brimming with pain and joy we can share.

For every single thing around us, even the bodies we hold dear,
are destined for the landfill.
Since only relationships endure, let us invest our hearts there.

RE-INHABIT LIFE

Every good tree bears good fruit, but the bad tree bears bad fruit.—
MATTHEW 7:17

---

*How do you pattern your day with habits to clothe
the passing moments of life?*

Renouncing the appetites of the marketplace,
the earliest monks
pursued the soul of Christianity into wild and rocky places.

In the desert they re-patterned life,
marking hours in prayerful rhythm,
into a daily office to transfigure routine into ritual.

Ironically, these ritual hours of office,
first formed in ancient cloister,
now shape the routine of office workers worldwide.

With due attention and wakeful wonder—
practicing soul-stretching habits—
mundane becomes mystical and work an act of worship.

The patterns of our lives reveal us. Our habits measure us. Our
battles with our habits speak of dreams yet to become real.
—MARY OLIVER, *Long Life*

How do we re-inhabit our days
to wear us wider
and stretch the span of our short sojourn?

Can we invest our brief time
in the sacred art
of becoming fully human?

What might shake us free from self-obsession
and bring us to our knees
as we negotiate the stumbling blocks of ideology?

And, if suffering-love is more lasting
than faith and hope,
what are we prepared to do, for love's sake?

And now these three abide, faith, hope, and love; and of these, love
is the greatest.—1 CORINTHIANS 13:13

The trust-filled gaze of an infant
implores us to do our utmost
to make a safer world.

Tender shoots, boldly up-reaching,
beckon us to stoop and tend to beauty,
green with hope's fullness.

Timeworn, aged hands,
shakily extended,
beg us to slow our pace and inhabit each fleeting moment.

Silent, hungry cries
of kin clad in different skin
fire the desire to simply live together as better beings.

This visible, earthly world is still God's creation: one should not
condemn it as a valley of tears; it is really the miracle work of
God.—EMIL BRUNNER, *I Believe in the Living God*

Try these soul-stretching habits,
re-solutions for re-inhabiting
every budding new year:

enter the dark quiet,
and listen for the signal
beneath the static;

seek sole time,
and turn off to tune in
to rhythms deeper;

extend loving attention
and cultivate concern for livelihood,
beyond the immediacy of you and yours;

practice Christhood
by letting everyone you meet today
know they are Christ-companions, not competitors in your way.

Whenever I groan within myself and think how hard it is to keep
writing about love in these times of tension and strife which may,
at any moment, become for us all a time of terror, I think to myself:

76

What else is the world interested in? What else do we all want, each one of us, except to love and be loved, in our families, in our work, in all our relationships?—DOROTHY DAY, *On Pilgrimage*

May you resolve
to shape a world
where it is easier for us all to love.

CHOOSE TENDERNESS

My servant will not break a bruised reed or quench a smoldering wick until justice reigns.
So that in this name will the nations find hope.
—MATTHEW 12:20-21

Can you envision the world that could be?

Another week, another season,
on our quest for rhyme and reason
while another day is born that many did not see.

As hours and eons run their course,
we make our spinning pilgrimage
and worry as we wonder:

Where are we all headed,
with such haste and fury?
What good newness needs to be ushered in?

Spirituality is about seeing. It is not about earning or achieving. It is about relationships rather than results or requirements.—RICHARD ROHR, *Everything Belongs*

Can we visualize a more loving global community,
peace-filled and forgiving?
Such re-visioning begs courageous imagination.

Imagination precedes realization,
for each fantastic new creation
is first conceived by imagining.

No longer need we resign ourselves
to self–fulfilling prophecies
that diminish care and damage life's fragile fabric.

No more must we glamorize violence,
glorify gain, or sacrifice God's precious children
to martial idols that manufacture death.

> Beloved, we are God's own children now; what we shall become
> has not yet been revealed.—1 JOHN 3:2

If we could just see
family in every face,
we might even love other children as our own dear ones.

Then, doubtless,
the crying needs of the living, in myriad form,
would trump the mongering and monetizing of fearfulness.

> From fear springs violence—yes, not the other way around.... Fear
> invented wars, weapons, and all the violence weapons can cause.—
> DAVID STEINDL-RAST, "With a Child's Trust"

It is love, and love alone,
that chases out fear.
And only deeper-wider belonging disarms hearts.

In the days yet to come,
each time life affords you the opportunity,
may you take the tender way.

May you speak with gutsy love,
from heart to heart,
choosing to forgive more readily, holding onto hurt lightly.

Once you start to awaken, no one can ever claim you again for
the old patterns. Now you have realized how precious your time
here is.—JOHN O'DONOHUE, "The Question Holds the Lantern"

In the brief, bright remaining moments,
with the limited breath you've been given,
may you speak your truth gently and forgive freely.

May you say "*Yes!*" to kin and kindness,
to listening, and listening more,
as you incline toward nature's meekness.

May tears tender you
as you tend
to your patch of fragility.

So, with the shine in your eyes,
may you bestow blessings unspoken
upon all you survey.

CROSS-CONTAMINATION

Moved inwardly with compassion, Jesus stretched out his hand and, touching the leper, said ... "Be made clean!" No longer could he openly go into any town, but he stayed out in the open and the people came out to him from every quarter. —MARK 1:41, 45

Have you ever been condemned for the company you keep?

Touching and being touched
by people lawfully deemed unwholesome,
Jesus shattered age-old taboos of ritual purity.

Now cast out,
he became accessible
to other hungry, hurting fringe-dwellers.

Choosing personal contact with "undesirables,"
he likewise consigned his companions
to the ranks of the contaminated:

untouchable, diseased, and distressed bodies;
dispossessed beggars; disgraced public sinners;
unseemly outsiders; and tormented souls,

for their condition forever condemned
to inhabit the outskirts,
beyond the margins of respectability.

Encircled by such discounted souls,
his vision, his message, his benediction
became virally infectious:

Blest are you,
already holy, freely forgiven.
Your lives matter!

Blest, too,
because you are listened to
and loved just as you are.

Blest even in your exclusion,
your craving for wholeness,
your longing to belong.

Though crushed and wretched you may feel,
you are also the hallowed
children of the Holy One.

Because you are hungry for justice, clear-hearted,
humble, mourning, poor, persecuted peacemakers,
you are warmly welcomed, presently blessed.

Thus, in scandalous solidarity,
with words, with wonders, with witness,
Jesus grated against the grain of entrenched meritocracy.

What fulfills for a moment is not worth the price of your soul.
—JENNIFER WELWOOD, "Renunciation"

Pilgrim beware the blessing
of this controversial Christ,
whose touch cross-contaminates;

whose vision beckons a bridge-building
Spirit that tolerates
no carefully constructed barriers to forgiveness;

whose friends
are sure to ruin reputations,
with guaranteed exclusion from polite circles.

Your very presence, now disturbing, your company
made contemptible, like your Teacher,
you are considered a menace to authorities political and ecclesiastical.

Following these tainted tracks of Jesus
inevitably leads to personal contact
with sullied and unsavory types

and surely bears the
promised, burdensome
bliss of persecution.

If these blessings have not
yet derailed you in discipleship,
you might well wonder whose lead you have been following.

There is no such beauty as where you belong;
Rise up, follow me, I will lead you home.
—MICHAEL DENNIS BROWNE, "The Road Home"

In this downside-up Reign of unlikely relationships,
the sinless, successful, and self-satisfied
are NOT the ones already sanctified.

Seeker, take care to befriend the Christ cast-aside,
not fearing the ruined résumé or blemished reputation,
but marked with the sign of cross-contamination:

God bless your head with understanding.
Bless your heart with love expanding.
Bless your arms with lives to tend,
with worthy work and wounds to mend.

HEARTS DISARMED

Peacemakers are blessed, for their name shall be children of
God.—MATTHEW 5:9

When was the last time your heart cracked open?

Children, our dearest-best tutors
draw out tenderness that softens calloused living,
evoking humble patience with invitations to be forgiving.

That primal urge to protect vulnerable life
calls out courage and care
in clearest reflection of our Maker Most Merciful.

Bearing witness to atrocious violations—
bullying, abuse, neglect, mass murder—
against God's dear ones, stirs rightful indignation.

No matter the depth of outrage
at the vile desecrations of violence,
the tools, tactics, and arsenal of domination cannot bring healing.

Armored, coarsened hearts foment aggression,
whetting a thirst for retribution
with oppositional posturing that feasts on fear-filled fragmentation.

> We are too tightly tangled together to be able to separate ourselves
> from one another either by good or by evil. We are all involved in
> all and any good, and in all and any evil....It is why God grieves and
> Christ's wounds still are bleeding.—WENDELL BERRY, *Jayber Crow*

First comes catharsis in lamentation,
a torrent which begs release
to break upon us and break us open.

Rachel must cry to the heavens,
and we must look each other in the eye
to make room for remorse, which alone transfigures suffering.

> In Ramah a voice is heard, lamentation and bitter sobbing. Rachel
> is wailing for her children; she refuses to be comforted, because
> her children are no more.—JEREMIAH 31:15

How else will minds be changed
if hearts cannot be cracked open
to let light come in and love pour out?

Without this change of heart—
fasting-weeping-mourning—
a nation infatuated with violence will find no peace.

How many more of God's precious ones
must be sacrificed
before altars of economic exploitation?

Abraham took up the knife to kill his son. From above, a messenger of the Holy One called out, "Abraham!... Do not lay a hand on this child, do him no harm."—GENESIS 22:10-12

There is nothing noble in the manufacture of death;
nothing moral in the marketing of mass destruction;
nothing peaceful in the weaponizing of citizenship.

What delirium equates life and liberty
with the unrestrained freedom
to market monstrous instruments of death?

Daily, across a nation
awash in destructive devices,
gun violence lacerates lives in city streets and school corridors.

Grief begs redress;
reconciliation requires admission of complicity,
the heartfelt desire to make amends to be made whole.

All your children shall be taught by the Holy One and they shall greatly prosper. In justice shall you be established; oppression shall be far off and you shall not fear; and terror shall not come near you.—ISAIAH 54: 13-14

Healing begins with the humble admission
of fallibility and gifts us with insight
into what it is to be human, what it takes to be holy.

Humbly we acknowledge our failure
to imagine safer, more compassionate
alternatives to life in these times.

Accepting that we are lost
allows us to be redirected
into fresh beginnings for a new time.

As disciples of the Prince of Peace,
may you follow that Peacemaking Spirit into creative tension
between grief (for what is lost) and gratitude (for new possibilities
given).

HOLDING FAST

Jesus was driven by the Spirit into the wilds to be tested by *diabolos* (the divider). There, for forty days and nights he fasted, and afterwards he was famished.—MATTHEW 4:1-2

What are you truly hungry for?

Hunger and thirst
are among the most primal drives in all creation.
What we hanker after betrays our truest motivation.

An ancient, ubiquitous practice,
fasting is easily misunderstood
in a culture of consumption.

Whether we abstain for labs
or medical procedures,
fasting always precedes some form of test.

Yet, unlike dieting,
with its measurable goals,
fasting extends an open-ended invitation into solidarity.

Such emptying-out invites non-attachment
and proposes a radical reorientation
of our relationships to life.

As full-bodied prayer,
fasting leads to physical desolation,
where we are sorely tempted

to gorge on spurious separations,
or lay bare our dependence
on the singular Source of all things.

Even now, the Holy One says, return to Me with your whole heart,
with fasting, with weeping, and with mourning; tear your hearts
open and not your clothes.—JOEL 2:12-13

Setting aside a personal appetite,
forgoing the appeal of a habit,
can allow gnawing awareness to grow into felt connection.

Far more than denial, fasting can be
the space-maker for the hopes and hungers
of famished neighbors, nations, and nature.

Resisting that drive to consume and control,
choosing incompleteness over satisfaction,
lets other struggles enter the belly of our lives.

And the empty hollowness we embrace,
that waits and wants to be filled,
holds possibility along with deprivation.

Out of that empty spot of silence where we feel helpless, embarrassed, and powerless, where we suffer from our own impotence to stop the reign of death in our world.

Out of those depths we cry...—HENRI NOUWEN

In the dank chill of this wintry world,
where greed, violence, and fear hold sway;
while we search hungrily for a glimmer of springtime;

may you lay bare your life
to the holy craving for merciful redress,
that aching appetite for the healing of all wrongs.

And may you make room for those most sorely afflicted
by exposing your heart to the parched desire
for deliverance, for restoration, and for peace.

You who hunger and thirst for justice are blessed, you shall indeed know fulfillment.—MATTHEW 5:6

UNLIKELY FRIENDSHIP

No greater love can you have than this, to lay your own life down for your friends.—JOHN 15:13

What do your friendships say about you?

Among mammals
we human beings are gregarious,
the most relational of the migratory species.

Though we muse and moan
about alone-time,
we are not natural solitaries.

From first breath to final gasp
we lunge outward,
ever reaching for togetherness.

All life long, we crave to belong.
Through our relationships,
we constantly calibrate who and how to be.

Drawn into intimacy,
we possess powers unmatched to bridge and bond,
despite difference and distance.

And through the eyes of caring companions,
friendly surrenders transform
the way we perceive this world.

Such friendships ferry us
beyond the harbors of language and ideology
and bear us over the maelstrom of class and culture.

From segregation, to congregation, to integration,
this is our homeward journey
toward the human wholeness of being 'with and part of'.

Friends live in the shelter of one another.—CELTIC PROVERB

Where and with whom we stand really matters
in this world-house divided,
so deeply carved, so many-sided.

Any friendship is a treasured gift.
Likely friendships happen;
unlikely ones never fail to surprise.

These less-likely relationships reveal character,
moving us from club to collective, committee to community,
and finally from solidarity into a circle of friends.

One of the tasks of true friendship is to listen compassionately and
creatively to the hidden silences.—JOHN O'DONOHUE, *Anam Cara*

In the hyper-individualized world,
"friend" and "community" are made plastic,
transitory, in essence transactional.

The burdens of commitment and co-responsibility
are off-loaded
whenever "like" usurps "love."

Technology lets us share images and messages,
yet ciphers and photons
are shallow substitutes for true human connection.

Only by keeping in touch
can friends find their bearings
and gaze at life together with the look of love.

Such befriending involves discipline
and demands cultivation,
a lifetime of keeping, tending, mending.

Friends must cover
the rough terrain of caring
if relationships are to ripen and bring sweetness to life.

Lasting friendship reflects
the golden distillation of matured relationship,
a sacrament that drips unanimity— a great soul shared by many.

Such soul friendship, priceless and rare,
is founded on vulnerabilities shared:
confessing, disappointing, breaking and remaking mutual care.

Likely or not,
our friendships illustrate, for all to see,
the cares and commitments that make us one and break us open.

In the end, it is the reality of personal relationships that saves
everything.—THOMAS MERTON, *The Hidden Ground of Love*

Friend to foreigners,
befriender of sinners,
caring for outcasts, for losers and winners;

friend of the earth,
of sky and sea,
friending the friendless and enemy.

This is how we follow the one
who taught us and showed us
how friends are to live and die for.

May you find your way
to let someone know
how much you mean to them today.

Chapter Five

Of Cycles and Seasons

O ur varied faith traditions are infused with profound apprecia-
tion for the rhythms and lessons of the good earth. This natural
wisdom shapes seasonal celebrations that mark the passing of our
years and reverence our "creature-hood."

As Christianity calcified, mind holding sway over matter, these
earth-bound roots withered. Now disembodied, "spirituality" retreated
into the conceptual realm of the psyche. A deepening suspicion of
nature reduced earth to "dirt" and considered indigenous and rural
people primitive. These degrees of separation, in turn, cleared the
way for the unrestrained exploitation of nature, treating creatures and
earthy human communities as expendable resources in the pursuit of
technological "progress."

The symptoms of centuries of deprivation and domination, our
increasingly synthetic lifestyles have now brought us to the brink of
global environmental catastrophe. And, nature-deprived faith has, in
effect or by neglect, sanctified the pillaging of God's good garden, a
precious inheritance for generations of creatures yet to be.

In such a time as this, how can the children of earth, sky, and sea
repair our relationships with all our fellow creatures, travelling
companions on our shared planet home?

Will we earthlings move from hubris to humus and live ourselves into a new way of being together?

Living slowly, with fewer compulsions.
Living humbly, demanding less.
Living simply, reducing our needs.
Living consciously, taking nothing for granted.
Living peaceably, blaming less and building bridges of reconciliation.
Living justly, tolerating fewer and fewer degrees of separation.
Living together and less apart, finding excuses to turn community into kin.
Living compassionately, shrinking the gap between our Maker's mercy and our care for neighbors.

LIVING ABUNDANCE

For where your treasure lies, there your heart will also be.
—MATTHEW 6:21

What keeps you grounded through the seasons of your life?

After decades of practice, studying the scales,
weights, and measures of an integrated life,
I have had to let go of almost everything I once held.

The heart is stretched through suffering and enlarged. But O the agony of this enlarging of the heart, that one may be prepared to enter into the anguish of others!—THOMAS R. KELLY, *A Testament of Devotion*

94

For a while, my pantheon
housed an array of minor deities,
each vowing to carry me closer to fulfillment.

Disciplines of asceticism, rigor and repetition,
devotional ardor, meditation and mindfulness,
philosophical argument, right action, and social concern

each took a turn on the podium,
pointing out pathways to perfection,
promising to uplift or nudge me further along.

Blessed be you, mighty matter, irresistible march of evolution,
reality ever newborn; you who, by constantly shattering our mental
categories, force us to go ever further and further in our pursuit of
the truth.—PIERRE TEILHARD DE CHARDIN, *Hymn of the Universe*

Now, at home with ample weaknesses,
I am spreading wide,
slowing like an aged river.

My desire to savor life,
in its myriad emanations,
has become prayer.

And knowing we have a brief time
to walk the soft grass together,
I intend to take my time and generously share it.

When seeds germinate,
roots come first,
drawn by gravity to penetrate earth's loamy heart.

In my ceaseless to-ing and fro-ing,
it is the grave
that draws me down.

Grave human realities
hold me here, weigh me, and draw me down,
rooted in place and time.

Life seldom disappoints
if we are determined
to stay awake and engaged.

Whether in tatters at the losses of the day,
or smiling at my own awkward antics,
abundance awaits.

I am delighted
by the fragrant bounty of wildflowers,
or the aerial gymnastics of swallows, open-mouthed in the wind.

Like all of us, I struggle with trying to control what happens and
trying to participate in what happens.—MARK NEPO

Gravity and levity, soul and spirit,
mind and body, wonder and woe,
there is room for this and more in a life slowly savored.

So, what makes for a well-lived life?
What is expected of us?
Have we not already been told?

...what is good; and what does the Most High ask but to do justice, and love kindness, and walk humbly with your God?—MICAH 6:6-8

Gratitude is the motive for justice;
mercy the courageous response to every situation;
humility the honest pathway into the fullness of humanity.

Abundant life reveals itself
the moment we cease
expecting, wanting, needing something else or more.

As we cycle through the mysteries
of living to die and dying to live,
may you take your time to suffer and savor life with those you love.

*Are you yet tender enough to be moved to mercy and
humble enough to welcome forgiveness?*

AUTUMNAL GRACES

Truly, I tell you, unless a wheat grain falls into the earth and dies, it remains just a single grain; but if it dies, it bears abundant fruit.—JOHN 12:24

Have you ever heeded the beckon of the fall?

With each autumn
we get to watch
earth wobble into winter.

And with each fall come lessons,
a harvest of graces
to color our lives and carpet the ground.

Let sky be glad.
Let earth rejoice.
Let the seas and all that fills them roar.
Let the fields and everything within them exult.
Then shall the very trees of the forest sing for joy...
—PSALM 96:11–12

As trees turn to fire,
nature announces her blazing revolution,
in showers ocher and orange gold.

If ever were offered three wishes—
as in the tales of children—
my desire would be for autumn's golden graces.

Three unexpected gateways to wholeness,
revealed in letting go,
falling down and giving-back.

What return shall I offer the Holy One
for all the goodness showered upon me?
—PSALM 116:12

If I could wish three graces for those I dearly love,
it would be these alone:
gratitude, tenderness, and humility.

Fruit of wonder,
gratitude is a gateway to joy,
turning lack, loss, and letting go into gilded gift.

Fruit of forgiveness,
tenderness opens the way to healing,
transfiguring pain into passion—love's long-lasting shadow.

Fruit of failure,
humility is the low door to wisdom
growing us back down to earth.

Mirroring the setting sun,
these autumnal lessons are poured out
in resplendent hues, for us to pore over.

Like all presents, they come to life in the unwrapping and the giveaway.
For every golden gift withheld surely turns to lead
and weighs us down with worry or woe.

We plant the seeds that one day will grow. We water seeds already
planted, knowing that they hold future promise...
—BISHOP KENNETH UNTENER

Perhaps there is a burden you are carrying.
Perhaps someone worries you.
Perhaps a situation weighs heavily upon you.

Welcome then, autumn's invitation
to grow by smallness and surrender,
by putting down, by giving away, by letting go.

There is no happiness without thankfulness,
no healing without hurt,
no wisdom without diminishment.

In order to possess what you do not possess
You must go by the way of dispossession.
—T. S. ELIOT, "East Coker"

When autumn slowly strips the landscape bare,
to surround us
in stark splendid death,

may we in thanksgiving
share the harvest,
and scatter the seeds of dreams to come.

And savoring the bounty of sunshine, showers,
soil, and sweat, may you seed peace, sow forgiveness,
leave the leaves, and let go!

WAKEFUL WAITING

And I say to all what I say to you: Keep awake!—MARK 13:37

As each year unfolds, what are you waiting for?

We call it longing
because it distends our sense of time,
and so much living is enlarged in the waiting.

Waiting...
    for healing to happen,
    anticipating a change to come,
    expecting a loved one's imminent return.

Waiting…
    for loss to soften,
    an ache to ease,
    a void to shrink.

Waiting…
    for tempers to cool,
    a chafed heart to mend,
    a conflict to ease, a bloody war's end.

Waiting…
    for a new day to break,
    a tired old one to wane,
    for the silence of night, or the chorus of dawn.

Waiting…
    for a newborn's cry,
    or a loved one's final breath;
    we vigil before the mysteries of birth and death.

Waiting…
    for the torrent to abate,
    eager for the drought's release,
    we hold out for hunger and injustice to cease.

So many ways
and shapes of expectation,
whetted keen in anticipation.

All the while, and all around,
so much secretly undeclared
quietly waits to be noticed, savored, shared.

The meaning of awe is to realize that life takes place under wide
horizons, horizons that range beyond the span of an individual life
or even the life of a nation, a generation, or an era.
—ABRAHAM HESCHEL, *God in Search of Man*

Endlessly empty,
waiting feels like drowsy,
mid-afternoon dullness.

Routines called "ordinary"
when taken for granted
numb and stultify.

Immune to golden sunsets and icy mountain peaks,
milky ocean spray and windswept wilderness,
we fail to notice the grandeur and beauty that over-wash us.

Even crisis fails to stir those still blind
to famished children, ravaged lives,
littered oceans, denuded hills, rapacious mines.

Daily life presents challenges and lessons
that measure our attentive presence,
and test our receptivity.

In every golden moment grace hides
in plainest sight
for those with presence of mind and a will to penetrate.

When life, love, or loss
lift the veil,
hearts and horizons are transfigured.

In the clarity of astonishment,
there is nothing
ordinary about existence.

Thus poets, artists, mystics come to life,
poised for inspiration,
to blow minds, crack hearts or mend them.

Attentiveness is
that heightened state of ever-readiness,
of wakeful watching and wondering.

Wakefulness sharpens connection,
disdains distraction, discards pretension,
unmasks self-preoccupation.

Like a statuesque heron intent on a gravelly stream,
or a tail-twitching tabby transfixed in the grass,
electrically charged anticipation sharpens senses with focus and
purpose.

Now we enter a state of expectant attention—
engaged presence—
the opposite of terminal boredom.

Fine-tuning the present, attentive to the peripheries,
scanning the horizon,
wakeful wondering disciples wait.

[God] came when the Heavens were unsteady,
and prisoners cried out for release.
—MADELEINE L'ENGLE, "First Coming"

Who knows how grace will
greet you this moment, this day, this year.
But will she find you awake and ready to receive?

LIVING FROM YOUR CORE

These people pay me lip service, but their hearts are so far
from me.—MATTHEW 15:8

Who calls you to be courageous?

When this whirlwind world compels you to rush,
patient wisdom urges you not to race,
but fearlessly to resist, pause, and gentle your pace.

And, no matter your stamina,
notwithstanding your station,
radical faith moves more slowly, with thankful determination.

Such deceleration announces your quiet revolution,
a deliberate return, in solemn resignation, to the meter of nature,
embracing her timeless truth: the deeper, the slower.

Patiently I waited for the Holy One, who leaned into me and heard
my plea.—PSALM 40:1

Winter teaches that the costly graces
of smaller, slower, grateful living
are borne of particular pains and personal hardships.

Yet wellness awaits
in unhurried, careful attention to being
that uncovers the miracle in each moment unfolding.

For faith let miracles appear.
Not rushing but resting; not seizing but receiving,
seeking out our reflection in the sacramental splendor of the universe.

In doing Your will I find delight, for Your law, resides deep within
my heart.—PSALM 40:8

Doubtless, we are living through a darkening season.
Tempest-tossed and torn asunder by tragedies and travesties,
we must first learn to lament our losses, desecrations, and
diminishments.

All around, diabolical shadows abound—
exploitative systems, rapacious economies, violent repressions of
tenacious life—
along with enduring love and fearless liberty.

But darker still is the obscurity within,
shrouded appetites and reflexes that give birth
to the desolation of careless, callous, cynical living.

Poor and needy though I be, the Holy One takes thought for me,
my help, my deliverer.—PSALM 40:17

In a communion of tears, shared grief gathers us,
giving voice, in sorrowful sighs, to our heartbreak at what is lost,
our gratitude for all that lingers, our hope in that which lasts.

Keenly aware that life is brief and sweetly precious,
the broken-hearted endeavor to slow down,
pay attention, and live from their exposed core.

For even winter's gloom
offers a quality of light,
a crisp-cold clarity that comes from having endured together.

> Courage is what love looks like when tested by the simple everyday
> necessities of being alive. —DAVID WHYTE, *Consolations*

Before our eyes, beneath our feet,
at the end of our noses and fingertips,
a universe of possibilities waits to be tended.

Paying attention to the life
that wheels around and swirls within
illuminates disaster, distress, and disease amid the wonders.

By daily and diligently finding ways
to express gratefulness for all life's graceful touches,
we are inoculated from corrosive cynicism.

Paying attention demands courage and takes time.
May you find your way
to calm the fears that drive you to distraction.

May you stubbornly refuse
to be rushed headlong,
but saunter through each day, heart-first and care-full.

Let not fear keep you from stopping
and stooping to touch and be touched
by the wonderful-wounded nature of life in these times.

FROM SEGREGATION TO INCARNATION

Be awake, stay focused, for you know not when the time will
arrive...—MARK 13:33

Who is sacred to you, and who is not?

We have entered that darkening time
of watchfulness,
a season of ripening contradictions.

Festooned with jingle-jangle,
temples of commerce lure us
with sweet indulgences so very good for the economy.

All the while, in hallowed spaces,
choirs croon
over starlit, snow-globe nativities.

So familiar are those alluring songs
and fuzzy festive feelings,
it is difficult to stay awake.

For unto us and into the fabric
of this deep-divided world, Christ takes fragile flesh;
God-within, all around, among us everyone.

Blinded by brutality,
carved up by inequity,
our fractured family huddles into separateness.

While some bow to the East
and others incline to the West,
we also hark from Global North or South.

And many undertake that desperate exodus,
crossing desert, sea, or mountain in search of peace:
possibility and the promise of a new beginning.

From ages past no one ever has heard, no ear has ever perceived,
no eye has yet seen any God besides you, who works on behalf of
all those who wait.—ISAIAH 64:4

It is so easy to divide us—
Dives from Lazarus, darker from lighter—
the handful who own more than the billions on the bottom.

With fanatic fervor some commit heinous crimes
in the name of merciless gods.
Others give their lives over to national supremacies.

And many millions more find their souls
somewhere in the middle,
worried and wondering.

It may feel safer to stay distracted,
to tune out distant gunshot terror,
disregard protest, hunger, horror.

We might even decorate our lives
with pious pageantry.
But wishful thinking does not bring peace to birth.

Into this world, this demented inn, in which there is absolutely no
room for him at all, Christ has come uninvited.

—THOMAS MERTON, *Raids on the Unspeakable*

Christ has not come
just for a few or some.
the Holy One wears the skin of everyone.

No fence or barbed-wired boundary wall,
no color, caste, or class,
can contain that merciful cascade meant for all.

For Christ bides with us already,
and we will know and be known,
when, as one, we refuse to be gated or segregated.

Under the rain of mercy
all are re-consecrated,
as separations are washed away.

In that blessed-broken body of Christ
there is no room for "they," no place for "them,"
and justice means "just us"—all and every one of us.

May you find your way today to honor the Holy One already
abiding-with-us.

HEALING SEASON

In the evening they brought many people who were possessed with malevolent spirits and he cast those spirits out with a simple word and cured all who were infirm. This fulfilled what the prophet Isaiah had foretold, "Our infirmities he took on, our diseases he bore."—MATTHEW 8:16-17

Who in your world is crying out to be heeded, holding on for healing?

To erect a barrier
or construct a divide
takes the effort of just one side.

Building a bridge will always require
foundations of trust
that both sides desire.

All who work with prophetic purpose
must beware the twin entrapments:
corrosive cynicism and coercive self-righteousness.

Desire for retribution,
no matter how justified its claim,
unleashes the diabolical profanities of blame and shame.

Conceding our commonalities,
receding into white-black boundaries,
steals space for understanding, depletes oxygen for dialogue.

To deny any possibility of restoration
only reinforces divisive systems
that fail to reverence complicity, connection, and care.

The greatest and most important problems of life are all in a
certain sense insoluble...
They can never be solved, but only outgrown.

—CARL JUNG, *The Secret of the Golden Flower*

Where might we sow the seeds of relationships
to sprout and surprise us with listening ears,
sheaves of shared sorrows, and the salve of outstretched hands?

The trajectory of Spirit, like radiant sunshine,
thrusts ever outward,
resplendent and reaching for communion, wholeness, generous
inclusion.

But we cannot envision what we do not see and
we will not heed what we do not hear,
until we hone the healing arts of love.

There is a season for everything in life, and a time for every matter
under the sky.—ECCLESIASTES 3:1

Radical resolution lies
in looking harder, listening longer,
with hearts agape at woe and wonder.

To outgrow the confines
of all we think we know,
we must plow the furrows of our longings and letting go.

Those willing to live
and love with abandon
will surely know the sting of alienation.

111

For we cannot splice spirituality
from humanity's deepest cravings
and darkest inclinations.

We begin
the new habit, getting up glad
for a thousand years of healing.
—SUSA SILVERMARIE, "A Thousand Years of Healing"

As you embrace your day contemplating care,
may you feel, in your bones, hurts and hungers
you can never fully comprehend.

Even as you taste sweet unanimity,
may you recoil at the bitterness
of discrimination and isolation.

Liberated to lovingly listen,
may your eyes widen to every unfreedom:
slavery, poverty, addiction, exploitation.

May your yearning for peace of heart
illumine in stark contrast
the failures of war and daily desecrations of violence.

Longing to belong, may your hospital home
welcome fellow pilgrims guised as foreign:
migrants, exiles without refuge or shelter.

May great-fullness season your soul
and inoculate you with warmth and humility,
leaving room around your table for the possibility of healing.

A Deeper Life

Put out into the deep and let down your nets. —LUKE 5:4

What draws you below surface events to plumb the depths?

The genesis of all our origin stories,
water is the pourable, potable miracle
upon which all known life depends.

At the very beginning... darkness shrouded the deep as Spirit
swept over the face of the waters. —GENESIS 1:2

Abundant on our wet world,
liquid water remains a rare resource
in the visible universe.

And while astronomers scour the stars for it,
countless women and girls in impoverished countries
make daily treks to rivers, lakes, or wells to collect water for their
families.

Water ceaselessly sculpts our life-scape—
filling ocean expanses, cavernous aquifers, and glacial snowpack—
as silently it slips in misty rivers through the air above us.

The water I will give will become a spring within... gushing up into
life everlasting. —JOHN 4:14

This life serum bathes our cells,
moistens our breath,
and lubricates our most joyful and excruciating expressions.

In its perpetual rising-up and raining down,
it mirrors the sacramental cycle:
outpouring forgiveness, transformation, and redemption.

From the stories of creation to the flood,
from the Red Sea and Jordan crossings to the Galilee shore,
our faith is saturated in watery images.

But let justice roll down like waters, and righteousness like an
ever-flowing stream.—AMOS 5:24

A potent symbol of our thirst for restoration,
cleansing water bears
life and death.

As ice melts and seas rise,
polluted streams
carry our flotsam out to littered oceans.

Fresh, clean water has now become
our most rapidly evaporating,
irreplaceable, and squandered gift.

For you my very soul is thirsting; my flesh is yearning for you, like a
parched land without water.—PSALM 63:1

Yet, water also mirrors mystery,
as still waters school us:
the deeper, the darker.

We are all capable of floating and sinking,
and we can choose to swim in the shallows
or strike out for the depths.

In the shallows, we move quickly,
though it takes effort just to stay afloat.
In the depths we are buoyed, upheld by the mystery beneath.

We are each created,
called, and capable
of looking, living, and loving deeply.

However storm-tossed
the surface of our lives may be,
there are slower currents in the deep.

When next you lift
a glass of water to your lips,
contemplate the miraculous elixir that shapes and showers us alike.

Whomsoever should give even a cool cup of water to one of these
little ones in the name of a disciple— I tell you truly, they shall not
lose their reward.—MATTHEW 10:42

Consider the invitation to slow down,
seek out connection, and be sustained by depth,
especially in the most disturbing tides of our times.

Chapter Six

Of Wandering and Welcome

As awareness deepens, our lives are enriched.

As love broadens, our hearts stretch.

As minds open, our kinship connections widen.

Wanderers, explorers, pilgrims, and wayfarers—we have always been a migratory species. From our nomadic beginnings to our treks across mountains, deserts, and vast uncharted oceans, our ancestors traversed every habitable continent of the planet. Natural curiosity, combined with an insatiable hunger for connection, still inspires explorations of the ocean floor, the stark face of the moon, and even the infinite, inscrutable expanse of the visible universe.

Across this world in constant motion, all of us hunger for acceptance and understanding. The epic journey has long been the archetype for our unfolding self-awareness. A deep yearning to belong lies at the heart of every spiritual pathway to fullness of life. This draw toward unanimity allows us to taste the intimacy of communion that we call "sacred" or "holy." Well-being is the fruit of welcome and inclusion, the commonweal that makes us whole. Estrangement and alienation stand in complete contrast to our lifelong quest and deepest desire for home and wholeness.

While our pilgrim planet makes her lonely circuit around the sun, consider the miles you have travelled in your brief sojourn. Call to mind the countless voyagers en route at this very moment (on foot, in the skies, in ships and vehicles of every kind), so many souls in transition, seeking knowledge, opportunity, safety, welcome, and that elusive state of being we call "home" that blends our "being" with our "longing" into belonging.

How do we heal our severed human family, so sorely divided, and make a home for the ones who have been cast out and cruelly isolated? Holy people make us feel at home. Pilgrims we all are, and hospitality, that prime virtue of every faith tradition, is the welcome that makes us well and opens the door to healing.

LIFE IS MOTION

In a dream, a messenger from on high appeared to Joseph and gave him these instructions, "Get up, take the child and his mother and flee to Egypt, and abide there until I tell you."—MATTHEW 2:13

If you had to, how far would you go to find safe haven for your family?

Ever emerging, erupting, evolving,
explosive creativity from boundless devotion,
life is miracle in constant motion.

No calculus or static system
explains this transubstantiation,
energy and matter in infinite re-formation.

Day unto day pours forth speech, night unto night declares
knowledge.

No speech, no words, no voice is ever heard;
yet their song resounds throughout the entire earth,
their words carry to the very edge of the world.—PSALM 19:2-4

Blizzards of spiraling galaxies,
upheld in cosmic flow,
slow dance to eternal rhythms that none can ever know.

Our swirling dust-mote planet,
in radiant eddy bright,
makes her endless circuit around a lonely light.

All on earth is mobile,
flowing river of relations,
as tides and seasons come, then go, without a destination.

The whole visible world is no more than an imperceptible speck in
the ample bosom of nature. No idea approaches it. We may swell
our conceptions beyond all imaginable space yet bring forth only
atoms in comparison with the reality of things. It is an infinite
sphere, the center of which is everywhere, the circumference
nowhere.—BLAISE PASCAL, Pensées

Ponder mass migrations
that very few will see,
of wildebeest and caribou, of butterfly and bee.

On grassy plain and foaming fathom,
clouded sky and forest floor,
living things on epic journeys stream and teem and ever soar.

Have you glimpsed those fast formations
riding high on tides of air,
undulating skeins of cranes that float from here to who knows
where?

A blade of grass is commonplace on Earth; it would be a miracle
on Mars. And if a blade of grass is priceless, what is the value of a
human being?—CARL SAGAN, *Pale Blue Dot*

And then our own dear story
speaks of a vagabond race,
compelled by such a sacred ache to find our one true place.

Empires forged now lie fragmented,
shards of shifting states, waves of exploitation,
spoils of conquest, war, and subjugation.

Who dares stem this human migrant stream
or shut out the refugee in flight
that hopes for hospitality, safe harbor from the storms of night?

---

you have to understand,
that no one puts their children in a boat
unless the water is safer than the land.—WARSAN SHIRE, "Home"

No barbed-wire boundary,
line or law, can coerce us to alienate
those who arrive in Christ disguise and stand before our gate.

The alien who resides with you shall be to you like a citizen in your midst; and you shall love this alien as you love yourself, for you too were aliens once, in the land of Egypt. —LEVITICUS 19:34

Now let the hinge of mercy creak,
and do your very best
to make a space at least for one, and pray for all the rest!

I was a stranger and you welcomed me. —MATTHEW 25:35

A FULLER FLOCK

As he went ashore, he saw an immense crowd; and he was inwardly moved with compassion for them, because they were like sheep without a shepherd; and he began to teach them many things.
—MARK 6:34

Who restores your trust in the kindness of humankind?

Listen, learn, be led!
This is how we come to know
who to love, how to serve, and as a faithful flock be fed.

On the crosswalk
I saw him
step right in front of me.

Head bent, as in prayer,
dark-hooded, ebony-faced,
bravely he flashed a look.

In one eternal instant
brown eyes met grey,
and what might be menacing appeared monastic.

I am at odds with all that requires me to be a symbol.
I insist on being real.—KATHY GALLOWAY, "Real"

Fear breeds mistrust,
presenting parasitic opportunities
to make some predators and others prey.

How many of your younger sisters and brothers
are daily endangered in predatory cities?
How much life is threatened by soulless predation?

And who will tend such troubled souls,
and attend to lives without opportunity or refuge?
Who cares for the trafficked, fragmented flock of the Holy One?

Beware pastoral pretenders, trapped in trappings,
who wield authority by blaming and shaming,
lambasting the lost, ignoring the wounded.

We too become predators
when we allow diabolical dread and rapacious greed
to carve us up and lead us astray.

The Holy One my shepherd is, I shall want for nothing.
—PSALM 23:1

Engaging deeper expectations, prophetic people meet rejection.
Persecuted by the presumptive powers they threaten,
they are caricatured as wolves.

Such prophets are not people ahead of their time.
They are simply single-hearted souls
who have penetrated the signs of these times.

Called in crisis,
they sound alarms with urgency,
but only because there is so much to be alarmed about.

How can modern Christianity have so solemnly folded its hands
while so much of the work of God was and is being destroyed?
—WENDELL BERRY, "Christianity and the Survival of Creation"

Sharply focused by the lens of faith,
their surgical critique illuminates what is not,
to highlight what and who we might become.

Prophetic people are truth-dwellers.
Gathering the scattered, they refuse to inhabit the gloom
by choosing to walk together toward what can and will be.

With medicinal mercy
they brew a tonic of hope
and begin to repair and rebuild what has been ruined.

May you embrace every prophetic opportunity
afforded you this day
to be folded back into this fuller flock.

One sea; many rivers.
One Love; many hearts.—NOEL PAUL STOOKEY, "One and Many"

NAMED AND KNOWN

He asked them, "But you, who do you say that I am?"
Peter answered, "You are the Anointed One."—MARK 8:29

Who are the nameless-labeled people in your daily interactions?

Human beings are name-givers.
Everything we encounter
receives its own unique designation.

From Higgs-Boson to Crab Nebula,
we confirm quantum and cosmic connections
with the gift of a name.

In sacred stories of our beginnings,
name-giving is a primal task;
our personal re-creative power.

Our earliest babbled utterances are names,
as we lay claim
to the critical relationships that shape us.

Like sails billowing in the winds of wonder,
consciousness unfurls
when we explore a universal ocean of connectivity.

The Universe is a continuous web. Touch it at any point and the
whole web quivers.—STANLEY KUNITZ

We plot our positions in life
using the names we confer upon one another
and every single thing under the sun.

Awareness of self and everything else
is held together by this
ever-expanding network of descriptors.

As we broaden and deepen our relations,
what was distant and unknowable
comes near and dearly draws us in.

Yet names are doubled-edged;
they can cut as well as connect,
narrowing or widening our field of vision.

Giving a name puts word to love—
or our lack thereof—
re-shaping the supple clay of reality.

We yearn to belong more than to be loved.—JEAN VANIER

Just as terms of endearment draw life close,
epithets, classifications, and categories
bruise or sever our sense of connection.

In our daily dealings, we can use this naming power
to distance, divide, and alienate ourselves
from the responsibilities of relationship.

What, how, and whom we name
determines our depth of integrity (our lived connection to life),
and describes the condition of our heart (our willingness to care).

The fewer collectives we adopt,
the closer we come to integrated living.
The names we choose, use and refuse, indict us all most honestly.

No one truly belongs in a category
or any other collection,
for alone and together, we are formed in mystery.

Yet how we hunger for intimacy,
even as we fear the risks of living deeply
and the costs of caring dearly!

Somewhere, deep within,
we sense that such connections and cares will change us,
free us from our need to be above and beyond.

In the Realm of Relationships,
Jesus refused title, rejecting office or distinction.
And, whether lawyer or leper, he called his followers by name.

There are no others.—RAMANA MAHARISHI

Naming is a first step into re-creation,
one way of expressing loving connection
without "they" or "them."

As we transition from purely transactional
to deeply relational living,
people and things are transformed from objects into subjects.

It all begins with one
simply difficult decision,

to let no one be anonymous and remain unknown.

So, we step out and into the Reign
by addressing every person and creature
with an acknowledgement of our fundamental connection.

Thus, named and known,
we can restore relationships
wheresoever fear and hatred have been sown.

STRANGER'S KEEPER

And will the Holy One not grant justice to those who day and night
cry out, or delay long in helping them? I tell you, God will grant
them justice and swiftly. But, when the Chosen One does come,
will they find any faith on earth?—LUKE 18:7-8

What will you tell your children's children about these tortured times?

The other day when Christ came by
holding her mother's hand,
   at the river's edge she started to cry
   on the bridge to a promised land.

When love of the law
supplants the law of love,
soulless bureaucracy blossoms.

As the faceless tyranny of legalism,
tears at the roots of co-responsibility,
it seeds an illusion of powerlessness.

What is legal commandeers what is moral,
conscience is conveniently circumvented,
ideology is idolized in fluttering emblems,

and anthems proclaimed,
with boast and bluster,
proudly belie their sullied ideals.

Calloused hearts are always cultivated,
rubbing salt into raw crevasses
that keep us torn apart.

All the while, the fate of our little ones
dangles dangerously
on the fickle whim of sentiment.

How can we not see the face of the Lord in the face of the
millions of exiles, refugees, and displaced persons who are
fleeing in desperation from the horror of war, persecution,
and dictatorship?—POPE FRANCIS, "Message for World Day of
Migration and Refugees," 2018

Yet, held within *compassion*
lies our *compass*,
and without it we quickly lose our bearings.

As there are always
profits in persecution,
so too are there prophets who speak for the children.

There is nothing more damaging to unanimity,
than the heartless disregard
of any soul estranged.

For this stranger's guise
the wounded Christ must use
to pierce our armor-plated hearts.

And once again the crying Christ-child
unmasks the naked lie of inhumanity,
robed in imperious authority.

The wolf with the lamb shall live,
the leopard beside the young goat shall recline,
the calf together with the lion and the yearling,
and a little child shall lead them all. —ISAIAH 11:6

In the clearing arc of history
who will you choose to befriend:
hand in hand with control and command
or lowly-led by childlike care, to welcome, love and mend?

TABLE SPACE

When you host a party, make sure you invite people who are poor,
as well as those who are infirm; who are unable to walk, whose
vision is impaired. —LUKE 14:13

What might radical hospitality look like in traumatic times?

The world begins at a kitchen table.
No matter what, we must eat to live.
—JOY HARJO, "Perhaps the World Ends Here"

Every beginning runs inexorably to conclusion.
And in the end, opposing factions and forces
all to the table come.

All conflicts,
whether familial or foreign,
inevitably end around some kind of table.

Let our hearts not be hardened to those living on the margin,
There is room at the table for everyone.—CARRIE NEWCOMER,
"Room at the Table"

Authentic prayer
cannot tune out
a chorus of cries and commotion.

It beckons us to lean in,
let in, and tune in
to life's symphony of expression.

From birdsong to train horns,
sirens to love songs, protests to gunshots,
verbal disputes to quiet kisses,

mindful presence excludes nothing.
It pulls up a chair
for the unexpected guest, wisdom, awareness, or perspective.

At the core of contemplation
resides a paradox:
the invitation to "restful dis-ease."

We settle into quietude;
we enter the silence
to listen closely to the world.

Prayer-filled people
do not absent themselves
from the thorny trials of our times.

If you dare approach the table
to present yourself in prayer, then attune your heart
to hallowed hope and hurtful grievance everywhere:

deep yearning for peace
in conflict zones
etched on tortured faces;

pleading people
traumatized
by cruel eruptions of violence;

huddled crowds
cradling flickering candles
in tragedy's wake...

Sooner or later,
we all long to be gathered
around a table wide, where welcome brings well-being,

where we might listen and learn
the meaning of mercy over sacrifice,
and what it truly takes to love every other.

Nor can we afford blindly and mutely to accept
daily dereliction and nightly violation
as unavoidable.

Within us
we all bear
some sharp splinter of discord and turmoil.

And we each hold
some measure of tenderness—
a head inclined, and a heart attuned to torment and tears.

When next your circle gathers,
set a place in the soft arc of your candlelight
for unexpected guests.

Holy is not narrow, nor is holy blind,
holy is boundless welcome
for any cast-out soul and all those left behind.

Therefore, get out there into the highways and by-ways, and invite
everyone you meet to come to the wedding reception.
—MATTHEW 22:9

No matter how you would define "them,"
will you hold open your heart and make a space
for the folk who live, or look, or love differently?

How we define the 'other' affects how we define ourselves.
—JOHN A. POWELL, "On Speech and Belonging"

And how else can we hope
to know and show
the unexpected peace of the uninvited Christ?

As you attend to the holy hunger you hold, whom do you
need to welcome to your table?

LIVE BY CONNECTION

Jesus said to the beggar, "What is it you want me to do for you?"
The blind man responded, "My teacher, let me see again." Jesus
said, "Go, your faith has restored you." Straight away, his vison
returned, and he became a follower.—MARK 10:51–52

How do you sort out the world that meets your eyes?

When someone approaches,
instinctively the self-protecting,
sizing-up begins:

attractive or awkward;
too large or small; unappealing or friendly;
frightening or forgettable;

places, people, and happenings are
strained through the personal filter
of impression and intuition.

This is how
we appraise the world
and make our way through life as it presents itself.

Daily we discern who merits attention,
decide which is weed or flower, pet or pest,
and determine whose lives deserve or bear lesser or greater import.

Thus, we pass our precious days,
sorting experiences and encounters
as we are carried along on life's ceaseless current.

We drift and sift,
taking in what appeals,
dismissing what appears distasteful.

A human being is part of the whole, called by us "universe," a part
limited in time and space.—ALBERT EINSTEIN

Whether ideas, events, or people,
we direct our life-energy
toward separating, selecting, affirming, rejecting.

It feels easier
to live by dissection,
rather than rooting out connection.

This driving instinct
to assess and categorize
serves a primal purpose.

Sorting and separating
helps us find friends,
meet mates, and protect ourselves.

But endless surface-sifting also

buttresses barriers, limits our lives,
and leaves us adrift in the shallows.

At the mercy of personal preference,
we miss other unfolding possibilities
that beckon from darker depths.

Contemplative living is living in true relationship with oneself,
God, others and nature, free of the illusions of separateness.
—ATTRIBUTED TO THOMAS MERTON

Living by separation—
who we are not and how we are different—
carves life into camps and collectives.

Deluded degrees of division—
skin tone, body shape, social standing, culture, politics,
wealth, merit—
invent false distinctions and invoke distance that allows us to
alienate.

So, we protect ourselves from the fundamental inclination
to care and connect with the plight and potential
presented in each encounter.

And who would dare defy categories,
reject the easy label,
or bring outcasts to our table?

Good News proclaims
an unrestrainable Spirit,
a connector with no respect for boundaries.

Mystics bear witness
to our deepest drive,
for intimacy and communion universal.

Spirituality affirms
a deeper hunger for wholeness,
an unquenchable thirst for unanimity.

Within divine diversity and distinctiveness,
we uncover a shared Source,
the characteristics of a profound connection to every other part of
the Whole.

Our task must be to free ourselves from this prison by widening
our circle of compassion to embrace all living creatures and the
whole of nature in its beauty.—ALBERT EINSTEIN

But how do we live by connection,
and reweave the frayed filaments
into a seamless whole?

Prayerful living thwarts fickle selectivity
and taking our bearings from compassion,
we are ever on the lookout for links, not lack or likes.

When gathered
in mindful presence,
we make room for the odd and the outsider.

We cast a wide welcome
to what seems lost,
forsaken, afflicted, estranged.

In our blessing power to consecrate—
to acknowledge together what is sacred already—
resides the potential to heal and transfigure the substance of life.

Any time we extend a blessing,
we affirm
our deepest, shared connection to holiness.

In fear-fueled times
it takes courage
to offer the hardest blessing of all:

> Bless your enemies and do good to anyone who despises you, bless
> the people who curse you and pray for those who abuse you.
> —LUKE 6:27

Will you be a consecrator, welcoming the world
through your wide-angled heart?

RECEIVE THE DAY

> Ask, and it will be given you; search, and you will discover; knock,
> and the door will be opened. For everyone who asks receives,
> everyone who seeks finds, and to everyone who knocks, the door
> opens.—MATTHEW 7:7–8

Are you aware of just how much has been given to you?

The way to wellness is found in welcome,
not in taking, seizing, grabbing,
but in humbly, graciously receiving and freely sharing every gift.

More than semantics,
the distinction between taking and receiving
demonstrates a foundational life orientation.

It is receivers not takers
who know the joys of sharing,
since what is well-received is more readily returned.

Cultivating a receptive heart
diffuses the bitter residue of entitlement;
that cultural compulsion to contrast, compare, and then complain.

Even when news is unpleasant,
we can receive without reacting;
holding hard-edged realities, to await their darker graces.

For the Holy One my soul waits, more eagerly than those who keep
vigil for the morning light.—PSALM 130:6

By rousing early, we point the way
to unwrapping the daily gift
with radical receptivity.

It begins, as the sky warms
from ocher to orange
with a wake-up glint of awareness.

Wonder ignites a glowing sense of awe
when silent luminescence
over-spills the lip of the horizon.

Thoughts widen

to welcome those ahead of us,
for whom the day has already ripened.

Echoed images from the evening news,
re-illumined by dawn, lead to wondering
about the challenges, struggles, joys that lie before us.

Countless beings
share this "now" along with us,
fellow passengers on our pilgrim planet.

It has taken nearly fourteen billion years
living, growing, hurting, healing, dying,
to get us to this particular moment.

Our lapses and losses,
wrong-turns and wanderings, distress and despair
are also part of this story unfolding.

Without anguished failure,
corruption, injustice,
we would not be who and where we are.

All existence stands in the dimension of the holy
and nothing can be conceived of as living outside it...
There is no escape from God!—ABRAHAM HESCHEL,
Man Is Not Alone

For us, this is a dawning threshold of the new day.
For others, it is a twilight of endings, long darkness beckoning.
For some the storm has passed, while others only sense the distant
rumblings.

For those ready to receive,

"now" is a fulcrum, between all that was and might be,

that presents pivotal questions:

How can we stare into the face of infinity and not be enlightened?

How do we connect this moment to the next?

How will we greet this day and handle its possibilities and

perils with care?

Every dawn brings tending and attending;

unexpected realities to embrace; tears and laughter to share;

conflicts to resolve; worries to hold; bodies, minds, and souls to

nourish.

But first, the deep breath before we plunge into presence.

On the brink of each bright moment,

let that initial exhalation be thankfulness.

Then, in darkness and in delight, we might proclaim with hearts

unhinged:

Thanks be to Thee,

Source of all we can see!

Chapter Seven

Of Earth and Spirit

Primal revelation, first catechist and original incarnation,
natural wonder of holy life is the Gospel of Creation.

To reconnect with blessedness at its most essential, we need only
contemplate the very first, most enduring revelation: the mirror
of our Maker that is so very, very good; and holy too in the redemptive
act of resting to celebrate and savor it. An ancient Bible tale tells of a
human family commanded to build a bark big enough to safeguard
every sacred being from the diluvium caused by human desecration.

Every creature belongs, each one is beloved, and none of us are
dispensable. Should we fail to appreciate and protect the likes of gnats,
lilies, and sparrows, how on earth could we even hope to taste and see
the goodness of their Maker?

Nature is also our first, best teacher who daily dramatizes, with
gentle meekness, the marvelous miracle of being. Witness how the
great mammals such as elephants, rhinos, gorillas, whales, despite
their bulk and strength, demonstrate delicate care as they tend to their
young.

As we make our annual pilgrimage around the sun, who could
know the uncountable stories of loves, losses, and longings—of tears,
terror, and tragedy—touched briefly each day in the passing shimmer

of sunlight. Deeper appreciations of the mysterious complexity of reality—at its most minute (in molecular and quantum dynamics) and universal (in the cosmic interplay of the galaxies)—continue to reveal an infinitely more intricate tapestry of mutuality and interdependence. Spirit breathes us into being and thrives on forever bringing us all back around to oneness and holding us all together, so we too can give ourselves to each other and know the real bonding of love, the infinite closeness of everything. In the end, awe remains the most honest response to new, surprising perspectives on the immeasurable breadth, unfathomable depth, and incomprehensible degree of our own unknowing.

GRACEFULLY GROUNDED

Other seeds into good soil fell and brought forth much grain, growing up, increasing and yielding up to thirty, sixty and even a hundredfold.—MARK 4:8

When was the last time your soles graced the ground beneath your feet?

Daily, we tread
or trample
a lush living carpet.

Upon this thin floor
of muddy vitality
all the elements of our existence depend.

What disdainfully we call dirt
(as in dirty) or soil (as in soiled)
is actually the miracle beneath!

People usually consider walking on water or air a miracle. But the real miracle is not to walk either on water or thin air, but to walk on earth. —THICH NHAT HANH, *The Miracle of Mindfulness*

Our given scriptural name
ADAMAH or "grounded one,"
describes our earthy roots and muddy origins.

Human reflects humble genesis,
for we are "humus-beings,"
earthlings realized from sacred soil.

The Holy One shaped *Adamah* from the dusty ground, and breathed life-breath into its nostrils. —GENESIS 2:7

Dirt is no dead thing.
Each topsoil ounce holds countless communities,
billions of invisible microorganisms.

One in four of the innumerable
forms of life on our planet
thrives in the dank recesses beneath our soles.

Unseen and unknown decomposers
recycle the necessary elements of life
until even deserts bloom in their season.

Earth purifies water, absorbs waste,
and, in the end, takes us all back
to remake our empty husks into life-givers.

Source of nourishment,
sacred soil provides raw material for reality
and cradles the bones of our ancestors.

Remove the sandals from your feet, for the place on which you
place your feet is holy ground.—EXODUS 3:5

When walking the woods
for the recovery of soul,
I cast my gaze upon the loamy litter scattered about me.

Such mucky wisdom, earthy lessons,
fruits, and seeds of innumerable seasons
lie strewn at my feet.

Earth's crammed with heaven,
And every common bush afire with God:
But only he who sees takes off his shoes.
—ELIZABETH BARRET BROWNING, "Aurora Leigh"

While living along the Amazon,
I was awed by the community of crawlers
that cover every available centimeter of forest floor.

To this day, the earthy aroma of wet leaves
carries me back
to amazing Amazonian epiphanies—

from our insect planet
rooted in a thin film of mud,
every imaginable form of breathing life erupts;

from towering mahogany to scarlet macaws;
in over-abundance
we have yet to name.

In our fleeting lifespan we are gifted
with a multitude of graces
in three dimensions:

Illumined Grace that gasps in wonder
at sunsets, ocean vistas,
and misty mountain peaks.

Darker Graces that visit us unbidden,
with the embrace of suffering:
the letting go and losing of all we hold dear.

Then there is Earthed Grace—
well-mixed into the messy mulch of living—
bounty revealed to the lowly, who live close to the ground.

Blessed are the humble, for they will inherit the humus.
—MATTHEW 5:5

With dusty hands and muddied feet,
may you know gratitude for the blessing of being wholly human,
graced to humbly walk God's good garden.

TOUCHED BY EARTH

God's Realm is like when someone scatters seed on the soil. Night
and day while they sleep and rise, the seed sprouts and grows;
how, they know not.—MARK 4:26-27

What does it mean to be rooted and grounded—
earth between our fingers, dirt beneath our nails?

There is no synthetic soul, no virtual holiness.
Neither by agency, nor rhetoric, nor reasoning
can we manufacture sacredness.

Holiness is free-gifted.
Sanctity presents itself,
the vital essence of every being.

But goodness, truth, and beauty
are graced to the gardener,
who has learned to embrace earthy wisdom.

For mercy rains down from heavy heavens,
justice erupts from saturated soil,
peace blossoms in the sublime harmony of living communities.

Life is too precious to permit its devaluation by living pointlessly,
emptily, without meaning, without love and, finally without hope.—
VÁCLAV HAVEL, *Disturbing the Peace*

Yet, so many of us earthlings
now find ourselves exiles
on our precious planet home.

Divorced from cycles
of sun and moon, seas, and soil,
we seem destined only to despoil.

Whether boxed in slum squalor,
where neither field, nor forest,
nor flower can grace our eyes,

or barricaded behind
artificial blinds,
where nature becomes a screen show,

our reverence is three times removed from raw reality
by heads distracted, hearts divided,
and hands calloused only from continuous clicking.

What greater stupidity can be imagined than calling jewels
"silver" and gold "precious," and earth and soil "base"?
—GALILEO GALILEI, *The System of the World in Four Dialogues*

Life herself, in proportions minute and monumental—
our singular bright sanctuary in the endless dark—
is soaked with sacred mystery.

When we no longer sense this sacramental presence,
we have traded our common birthright for "urbanality"
and lost our way back home.

How sad to separate
our souls
from the good green earth,

to desecrate the sanctity of soil
and denounce salt of the earth people
as dirty, pagan, heathen, villain.

For followers of a meek Master,
once a worker of wood,
touching earth is our spiritual, human practice.

By calling us to consider the lilies, the ravens, too, and sparrows,
our teacher was taught by nature
to renew the covenant with creation.

Reconnecting with the loam of our lives,
we learn that holy is not heavenly.
It is in the humus of our humanity that we touch the grain of mercy.

That Christ may dwell in your hearts through faith, as you are
being rooted and grounded in love.—EPHESIANS 3:17

And it is to the crumbled communion
of countless ancestors under our soles
that every single body is commended.

Will you stoop today, be touched by sacred soil,
and therein sense the silent stirrings of spring?
Nothing is more critical and urgent for us than
growing deeper down.

In the wilds the pastures overflow,
the hills gird themselves with joy,
the meadows clothe themselves with flocks,
the valleys deck themselves with grain,
all shout and sing together for joy.—PSALM 65:12-13

Blessed are you, who wake up to this unfurling Realm,
to till and tend and be touched by resilient soil,
wherein we plant the seeds of possibilities unforeseen.

NEARER AND DEARER

Look at the fig and all the other trees; as soon as they sprout leaves
you can see it and you can tell that summer is coming near. So too,
when you see these things taking place, you know that God's Reign
comes close.—LUKE 21:29-31

What kind of mystic are you?

Caught in reality's brilliant glare,
blinded by our headlights, we stare
at the mess we have all manufactured in this world.

The portal to understanding
the signs of these times
ever eludes our muddled minds.

For Wisdom takes a darker route,
from head, to heart, to guts and out
to mystery, so far from the tiny kingdom of our knowing.

The Christian of the future will be a mystic or will not exist at all.—
KARL RAHNER, *Theological Investigations*

Mysticism is neither magical, nor is it beyond us.
We each possess innate capacity for the deep, caring connections
that liberate us from self-imposed isolations.

Any death, small or great, is guaranteed to do it,
perhaps also a piercing daybreak;
the warm embrace of a long-lost love;

haunting music, booming surf at sunset, a mountain vista;
a courageous smile, a warm tear,
or the trembling touch of another who is suffering.

Each encounter, warmly welcomed,
can puncture our delusions of separateness,
drawing us down into the well of intimacy.

I fall. I get up. I run from you. I look for you.
I am again in love with the world. —MARK NEPO

In such mystical moments,
we are penetrated, and boundaries burst,
as we sip and savor that broader fullness of being.

And the closer we are drawn toward the Holy Hub,
the nearer we are brought to all,
and every manner of thing.

This includes painful losses, neglect and apathy,
along with the joy-filled bliss of children,
and the fresh spring rains, precipitating possibilities.

Though we start our growing up
learning to live by dissection—
defining differences, marking separations—

we end up growing down into connection,

seeing through porous delineations,

dissolving back into our foundational oneness.

Each of us is as old as the universe and experiences our greater self
in the larger story of the universe. So we are as old as the universe
and as big as the universe ... We exist eternally in our participation
in the universe's existence.—THOMAS BERRY, *Selected Writings*

Most often, mysticism catches us unaware.

What would happen to our relationships to life

if we wanted, willed, and welcomed such compassionate connections?

Perhaps that Holy Realm which,

in parable and paradox Jesus illustrated,

is that very state of being nearer and dearer to everyone and

everything.

Could it be that all we need

to wake up to this reign of intercommunion

is to be receptive—hungry enough for it?

We are already one. But we imagine that we are not. And what we
have to recover is our original unity. What we have to be is what we
are.—Thomas Merton, *The Asian Journal*

May you let compassion

come close enough

to carry you out and away.

WAKE UP TO WONDER

Consider the ravens: they do not sow, nor do they reap, they have
neither storehouse nor barn, and yet God feeds them all.
—LUKE 12:24

What wakes you up to the hidden touches that grace your days?

If you are blessed
to wake up warmly
under soft clean sheets,

conjure the sun-drenched cotton,
gathered, dyed, and woven in places
where nimble fingers and sweat come cheaply.

For there are others
who emerge after sheltering under a bypass,
wreathed in cardboard, nestled in yesterday's news.

The hiss and rumble of natural gas
ignited in your furnace is nature's gift,
gleaned from petrified, primeval forests that now release their
long-coveted sunlight.

Consider the once-green hilltops,
blasted-bare and gouged by hungry machines,
and mountain communities that rely on this predatory production.

In order that we might live, stars in their millions, tens of millions,
hundreds of millions even, have died. The iron in our blood, the
calcium in our bones, the oxygen that fills our lungs each time

we take a breath – all were cooked in the furnaces of stars which
expired long before the Earth was born. —MARCUS CHOWN,
The Magic Furnace

You step into a steaming shower,
refreshed by waters from lakes and rivers re-directed,
piped and purified.

Remember too, that clean water
remains beyond the reach of millions
who trek daily to standpipes and muddy waterholes.

Wreathed in underwear crafted in Bangladesh,
denim from Nicaragua, leather molded in Malaysia,
you are swathed in the weary handiwork of the world.

Now you cradle your morning brew,
harvested in Sri Lanka or Guatemala,
held in a mug fired in a Chinese factory.

You smear your breakfast bread,
baked in a far-flung city,
with summer fruits, gathered from fields unknown.

And, savoring the rush of sweetness,
you reflect on other hungers unabated:
for warmth, food, friendship, dignity.

Before even stepping outside to draw in
the morning freshness with the canticle of the birds,
already you are gift-wrapped in the wide world.

When we try to pick out anything by itself, we find it hitched to everything else in the Universe. —JOHN MUIR, *My First Summer in Sierra*

As you slept, a multitude of unseen hands
worked the land, shifted boxes, mined minerals,
and manufactured the material of your morning,

while the good Earth relinquished
her bounty of soil, showers, winds, and winding rivers
that make this and each passing moment possible.

Radioactive radiance enlightens your morning
with the realization of the ageless interplay of matter and energy,
travail, and tragedy—
the ceaseless cycle of passion-death-resurrection.

Spidery filaments
of mystery, misery, and magnificence
all entwine to entangle us in the morning's first communion.

This tracery of holy connection is revealed by dewdrops,
shimmering breezes, and sparkling sunlight,
along with the frantic flapping of life, trapped in tragedy.

When next you step into the web of morning
wearing the world and wondering about the Source of All Being,
may your heart swell with gratitude for each blessed momentary
connection.

So shall I bless You as long as I shall live;
I will raise my hands and call out Your name. —PSALM 63:4

Only those who know
how blessed they are
can be a blessing to others.

WIND AND FLAME

And again, Jesus said to them, "Peace be upon you. As Abba sent
me, so I now send you."
After saying this he breathed over them and said, "Receive the Holy
Spirit."—JOHN 20:21-22

*Are you hoping for peace and quiet, hungering for peace
and justice, or both?*

Let us be still,
slow to a stop,
rest, and be restored.

Daily we must relearn
to hand over the demands of the day,
inhaling deeply fresh air laden with re-creative possibility.

How do we find those restful latitudes
where we gratefully pour life's leftovers
back into the lap of Our Great Lover?

Some find solace on the meditation cushion;
other disciples seek out the Calmer of Storms
who calls us to wander the lonely places.

Come away with me to a deserted place all by yourselves and rest
for a while.—MARK 6:31

Yet, once awakened,
attuned to cries of affliction,
we are not inclined to slumber.

Why do our hearts not burst with sorrow
at the litany of lamentations?
Where is the indignation to mobilize the masses?

To care is to connect
and feed the smoldering desire for change—
the hot hunger for hope.

As he approached the town gate, a dead body was being carried
out. He had been the only son of his mother who was herself a
widow; and there was a large crowd. Seeing this, the Teacher
was moved deeply with compassion. "Do not weep," he told her.
Stepping up, he touched the bier and the bearers stood still. Then
he said, "Young man, I say to you, arise!"—LUKE 7: 12-14

But do we really care
enough to be touched, charged,
and to change the way we live our days?

Does not love burn
with urgent ardor to heal
and help upturn the skewed tables of torment?

Some would mold
this righteous restlessness
into a torch,

calling upon the sun of justice

to drive the death-dealers
from our earthly sanctuary.

Ours is no airy faith.
Nor is it only
ardent anger for action.

Flames need oxygen,
and the winds must
be warmed for movement.

Without air, the fire burns out.
Without fire,
wind dies in the doldrums.

As the heart is restored
even in its ceaseless rhythms,
can we not also find restoration in our rousing?

Feeding the fire, warming the air!
The world can scarcely
afford drowsy disciples.

Nor dare we expend our fuel
on what fails to satisfy,
forgetting to pause, ponder, and conspire.

Tongues of fire come
to rest AND to rouse,
for we are bound together,

folded into ONE,
you and I,
by a raucous-spacious Spirit.

With absolutely no respect
for locks, bolts, and boundaries—
lacking limits and loosening tongues—

we are impassioned
to speak peace to each heart
and breathe openness to every confinement,

to heat lukewarm hearts
and stir up
a storm of creative opportunity.

I want to be famous in the way a pulley is famous,
or a buttonhole, not because it did anything spectacular,
but because it never forgot what it could do.
—NAOMI SHIHAB NYE, "Famous"

May you be touched and transformed
by that restless-peaceful passion of Pentecost.
God knows, the world needs it!

Bless you Most Holy One ...
who makes the winds into your messengers,
fire and flame your ministers.—PSALM 104:1, 4

FROM SCARED TO SACRED

Fear not little flock...—Luke 12:32

What frightens you most these days?

As a timid child,
I was fearful of
many things.

Impressionable and imaginative,
I conjured monsters
from darkened corners and curtained windows.

Loud noises, thunder,
fireworks, and fire engines
all sent me into a panic.

It was mostly ridicule and shame
that motivated me to master
those childish nightmares.

You need not fear the terrors of the night,
nor the arrows that fly by day.—PSALM 97:5

Yet fear is not easily dispelled.
Instinctual and intuitive,
it triggers ancient alerts to protect us.

And we are magnetically attracted
to images and experiences
that stimulate those primal sensors.

In great measure, pressed down and overflowing,
fear is the currency that information peddlers dole out daily
to insatiable mass appeal.

And there is reason to be afraid:
global climate change, exploitation of life and lives,
weapons of unimaginable destruction...

We can afford
neither to ignore nor indulge
fear-filled nightmares and desolate predictions.

When we are frightened
we hide, huddle, and hold back
with tight-locked hearts, behind barred doors.

Suspicious self-protection
erects an unassailable bulwark of absolutes
to keep us safe.

And within these dungeons of our own design
the expanses of mystery, gratitude, abundance, deep listening
are placed beyond reach, on the other side of a steel-cold door.

So we are left with the bitter fruits of fear:
segregation, stockpiles, starvation,
and spiritual asphyxiation.

As a covenant to the people have I given you; as a light to the
nations, to open blinded eyes, to draw out captives from their
dungeon, and from the prison those who sit in darkness.
—ISAIAH 42:6-7

Fear is a most potent motivating force,
and our religious institutions
are not immune to it, nor do they shy from using intimidation.

Fear-driven communities are:
focused on command and control;
rigid and self-referential; drawn to condemnation;

arid and deprived of creative diversity;
unwilling to embrace moral complexity;
suspicious of free spirits.

When we suffer from such spiritual sclerosis,
it helps to keep in mind that "church" was born
in just such an unlikely place.

The gate-crashing, fiery, and feral Spirit
launches us
on an ongoing healing mission of restoration.

It lifts us over any barricades of ideology or theology
that would seek to separate God's children
from the oneness of creation.

All who cooperate with this Spirit of Oneness
are drawn out
by an ever wider, ever deeper love-force.

For the liberated soul,
it is much more vital to be transformed
than to be vindicated.

We can, to a certain extent, change the world; we can work for
the oasis, the little cell of joy and peace in a harried world. We
can throw our pebble in the pond and be confident that its ever
widening circle will reach around the world.
—DOROTHY DAY, "Love is the Measure"

What might you do today, and where might you go, if you were fear-free?

WILD AND HOLY

Immediately the Spirit drove him out to the wilds. In the wilderness he was tested for forty days by the Evil One and he kept company with wild beasts while angels waited on him.

—MARK 1:12–13

Where do you go to encounter nature's holy, healing touch?

Deprived of natural habitat,
we retreat into the head
to feast on flashing images and make ideas our daily bread.

No creature
is designed or created
to be caged.

All were made
for the wide open:
freely to roam, broadly to range.

The magnetic majesty of creation
exerts a hold on our soul,
not merely as a playground, but as our living room.

God is at home; it is we who have gone out for a walk.
—MEISTER ECKHART

The wilds and woods
still have the power to enchant and captivate,
for we but recently clambered down from the trees.

By walking leafy woodlands,
we break free of our heady hermitage
and come back to earth where all belong.

How can we know our own creaturehood
unless we bask in our relationships
with the soil and seasons of our natural neighborhood?

The moment we step outside,
draw breath, and walk into the wild,
we are observers no longer; we are participants.

The Real Prayers are not the Words, but The Attention That
Comes First.—MARY OLIVER

Failing to thrive in artificial isolation,
sterility breeds synthetic spirituality—conceptual ideology.
But we grow whole in spirit, grace, and body when grounded in
earthy relationships.

Denied daily natural connections,
our human nature is distorted.
The "development" of urban devastation testifies to the alienation of
people from planet.

Consider the multitudes,
brothers and sisters all,
consigned to shantytown or defined by suburban sprawl.

As nature-deprivation deepens,
our family, named for earthy humus,
dwells dislocated in a concrete wilderness.

Ever-expanding mega-cities foster fearful amnesia
about our sister species, till we forget that all who creep,
swim, or fly are treasured companions on Thy Holy Mountain.

These neighbors have so much to teach,
to ground, and keep us humanly holy
—imaged in the One who made all of us.

Uncountable are your works, Holy One!
In wisdom you fashioned them all;
earth is filled with your creatures.—PSALM 104:24

Pilgrims on this planet,
we root for connection,
our own place in the expanding universe.

Timeless rocks, endless stars, expansive ocean depths,
majestic hills, transient insects—living parables all
and facets of the Life that lives through us.

Should we ever pay attention,
creation will oblige with magnificent demonstrations
of gentleness, generosity, tenacity, and release.

Without the teachings of figs and fungus,
of rocks and worms and wrens,
how shall we come to know the cycle of life everlasting?

This grand show is eternal. It is always sunrise somewhere; the
dew is never all dried at once; a shower is forever falling; vapor is
ever rising.—JOHN MUIR

Pilgrim, you are here to appreciate magnificence!
And justice always paves the way for beauty,
the truest trademark of our Maker.

You have power in your holy hands
to bring justice back to each relationship
and imitate the grandeur resplendent in creation.

May you go out of your way today to let nature school your soul
and restore your holy humanity by drawing you near
to the One at the heart of it all.

Postlude

A new commandment I give you, that you love each another. In the same way I have loved you, you also should love one another. In this way all will know that you are disciples of mine, by the love for one another you have among you.—JOHN 13:34-35

Seeker,
In the transience of time, your life is far briefer than you realize. Who can tell what tomorrow might bring to any of us? And tomorrow itself is always, by its very nature, insubstantial—not ever a real thing.

So, while still there is breath in our bodies and there are tears in our eyes, let us not waste any opportunity to let the world know how in love with life (and every expression of it) we are, how very good it is to be here together, and how much, how deeply we love one another.

BREATHLESS

The wind blows where it chooses, and you hear the sound of it, but you know neither whence it comes nor where it goes. So it is with everyone born of the Spirit.—JOHN 3:8

When was the last time life left you breathless?

Amazonian forest-dwellers
taught me a gentle exercise
in expansive presence.

Standing silent with eyes peeled
and ears attuned,
you drink in the surrounding sensations.

No longer an observer,
you let yourself be welcomed back,
wrapped into the woods.

In wordless conversation with the chattering redwing,
glistening turtle, shivering doe,
you hear the breeze blow through you with every breath.

An inch of surprise leads us to a mile of gratefulness.
—DAVID STEINDL-RAST, *Gratefulness*

These days, creation comes to visit me
in my urban exile,
anytime I pay closer attention.

I cannot help noticing
crabgrass cracking concrete,
and clouds of moths dancing in orange streetlight glare.

A blue skink tail disappears under trash,
a phoebe shouts her name from a locust sapling,
and the dark, silent sweep of a turkey vulture dissects the blue.

Without trying, I am awakened,
caught breathless,
surprised by all that comes out to greet me.

Like Virginia Creeper gently reclaiming an abandoned home,
nature's green force relentlessly encroaches,
and I am astounded by the wildness I mistook for a desert.

You do not need to know precisely what is happening, or exactly where it is all going. What you need is to recognize the possibilities and challenges offered by the present moment, and to embrace them with courage, faith, and hope.—THOMAS MERTON, *Conjectures of a Guilty Bystander*

Once, someone asked me how I pray,
what techniques I used,
and who were my masters of meditation.

Embarrassed by the question,
I was too self-conscious to admit
that I am not really sure whether "I pray" at all.

Perhaps it is more honest to explain
that prayer happens to me,
and I cannot help it.

After decades dedicated to meditative mechanics,
life wore me down
till I gave in to the gravity of the present.

Thus eroded, and standing saturated in the moment,
prayer happens by breathing, listening,
noticing, waiting, and watching.

Is this technique?
It evades description, except to say that
showing up without another agenda, prayer overtakes me.

This can be most inconvenient, even annoying,
interfering with driving, making supper,
washing up, and interrupting writing.

When I find myself captured
in quiet communion with life,
smiles erupt or unsolicited tears well-up.

I exchange knowing glances,
even whispered greetings,
with plants and animals, clouds, and crowds of people.

Perhaps I am undisciplined,
more delighted than enlightened
by the nature of prayer that captivates me.

As wise teachers have demonstrated,
the span of life is not measured by the number of breaths taken,
but by the breath stolen gasping at nature's grandeur and the sea of
suffering that surrounds us.

How freely do you give your breath away?

LOST AND FOUND

Rejoice with me, for I have found my sheep that was lost.
—LUKE 15:6

Who looks out for you?

We need not look far and wide
for the Source of Being, around and inside
since Presence relentlessly seeks us out.

The surprise of salvation is that we are all headed for healing,
pursued by Mystery,
found in forgiveness,

by an ever-patient Presence who,
unperturbed by waywardness,
tenaciously tracks us down.

Whence could I flee your Spirit or escape your Presence?
—PSALM 139:7

For a time, we might cast ourselves
into the chasm of mass distraction,
thinking to be unreachable.

For a while, we might let our souls be held captive
by the shadow-play of plasma screens,
or gorge on sound-bite reactions to life's tragic wonder.

But, in due time, even here,
joy can unseat us, mystery unsettle us,
pain up-end us, and forgiveness find us out.

Every seeker understands
what it is to be found and found out,
sought and caught out by life.

Awe enables us to perceive in the world intimations of the divine,
to sense in small things the beginning of infinite significance, to
sense the ultimate in the common and the simple; to feel in the
rush of the passing the stillness of the eternal.
—ABRAHAM HESCHEL, *God in Search of Man*

Those on a quest
are content to be enticed into unknowing
by penetrating questions.

And the lonely soul
finally finds home
by welcoming others.

> Whomsoever welcomes you welcomes me, and welcoming me,
> welcomes the One who sent me. —MATTHEW 10:40

And should we allow ourselves to be found,
we might receive and radiate mercy,
becoming bright beacons in the densest night.

We cease pursuing a separate "Other"
when we are entangled,
caught up in the hurting-hope of a sister or brother.

New-found by forgiveness,
the hungers of the sorely afflicted among us
unshackle us from spiritual self-seeking.

Forgiving brings us to our knees,
not to beg but to revere,
to let ourselves be found, without trace of shame or fear.

Holiness is no longer hidden, except in plainest sight.
Joy kindles hearts,
and hope hangs on every smile.

> If only they could all see themselves as they really are. If only we
> could see each other that way all the time. —THOMAS MERTON,
> *Conjectures of a Guilty Bystander*

Afterword

Christian spirituality proposes an alternative understanding of the quality of life and encourages a prophetic and contemplative lifestyle, one capable of deep enjoyment, free of the obsession with consumption.—Pope Francis, *Laudato Si'*

Do you realize how truly blessed you are?

Joy is infectious. It cannot be withheld or meted out in meager portions. Like love itself, joyful generosity is measured not by how much we give out, but by how little we hold back. It is the juice of loving justice, sweet nectar squeezed from the plentiful fruit of the Spirit of Wholeness. It is savored, freely showered and shared by those who know and understand just how much they are blessed. Their kind of blessing, however, has little to do with fortune, prosperity, popularity, or success. Its bounty is shared by those humble enough to know their own poverty, who are mourning and merciful, who are clear-hearted, peace- and justice-makers—those who have known persecution.

These unexpected beatitudes uncap the well of joyfulness within, allowing us to revel in the simplest beauties of everyday living. Not to be confused with superficial or artificial attraction, beauty can be found in the smooth face of a child, the knotted hand of an elder, or the bravery of a single weed, breaching the concrete-clad desolation of an abandoned lot. Beauty is ubiquitous, though sometimes we have to search or even squint to find it. And we cannot live well without beauty. It inspires, it heals, and it is abundant. Joy-filled beauty escapes through the crack of our smile, the chuckles of a child, the skylark's song, and the shine in our eyes. Like pain, beauty also blesses us by perforating our surface perceptions to open a skylight in our self-protections and preoccupations. This blessing power is a love-force capable of transforming how we receive and respond to whatever comes our way, and whoever crosses our path.

May you be touched this day by the contagious joy of knowing just how blessed you are.

JOY UNBRIDLED

I have told you all this so that my joy may reside within you, and your joy might be whole.
—JOHN 15:11

When was the last time you laughed till you cried,
or cried till you laughed?

If ever you forget what joy feels like,
imagine walking with a finger-clutching toddler
squeezing delight from every encounter.

Dwelling overlong in the dark,
by insufficiency and inconsistency beset,
leaves us paralyzed in suffering, hobbled by regret.

Tired disappointment dampens the embers of joy.
In this world there is pervasive injustice, violence deep and dark.
Evil is real, but so too, and even more so, is radiant love.

How lovely upon the mountain are the feet of the messenger who announces peace, who brings joyful news, who proclaims healing restoration, who declares, "Your God rules!"—ISAIAH 52:7

The gravity of justice and the lightness of joy intertwine
when we renounce the restless pursuit of pleasure
to engage with others in their struggles and celebrations.

If the fruits of justice are ripened in relationships,
righted and restored,
then joy is that sweet nectar pressed from friendly community.

How sweet it is when kinfolk live together in harmony
—PSALM 133:1

Only in such closeness
can we envision and embrace a Spirit joyful,
casting the wide world in a wholly different hue:

with iridescent wonder, resplendent forgiveness,
touching tenderness, salty tears, infectious laughter,
and a pulsating nearness to everything.

Joy is the serious business of heaven.—C. S. LEWIS,
Letters to Malcolm

Unbridled joy mirrors the Divine heart.
Coupled with gladness, it sparkles,
glistening and jewel bright.

Not to be confused with fun,
joy is unselfconscious, outgoing,
touching, and tickling all within reach.

This distillation of friendship
rushes out to meet us
each time we revisit our real kinship with creation.

Let us sing as we go. May our struggles and our concern for this
planet never take away the joy of our hope.
—POPE FRANCIS, *Laudato Si'*

While we can reflect its light—
sup and savor, rejoice and enjoy—
we cannot manufacture an essence not sourced in us.

Like unfettered grief, unbridled joy leaves us beside ourselves.
When we wade through the sorrows of life together,
joy can also reclaim us.

It is ours to give in to and give away.
Conduits, not containers, are we
who do not keep it, but transmit, reflect, and set joy free.

The fullness of joy is to behold God in all.—JULIAN OF NORWICH,
Revelations of Divine Love

Joy leaks out when
least we expect,
quietly through the corners of mouths and moist eyes.

Announcing itself in back-slaps and belly laughs,
it shimmers in the secret glances
between lovers.

Have you glimpsed it shining in children, frolicking at the shanty-town spigot?
Have you heard it announce itself in the morning psalms of the birds,
or resonating in the beggar's subway soul-song?

Joy is the infallible sign of the presence of God.
—PIERRE TEILHARD DE CHARDIN

May the Source of All Gladness
gift you with unbridled joy this day,
so that you might kindly bless all you pass along the way.

And may light shine out of the two eyes of you,
like candles set in the windows of a home,
bidding the weary wanderer come in out of the storm.

—GAELIC BLESSING, ADAPTED

About the Author

A native of Scotland, Joe Grant received a Master of Divinity degree from Catholic Theological Union, Chicago. He has served as a missionary and minister in Europe, the U.S. and Latin America. As Director of Programs for JustFaith Ministries, he created nationally recognized formation processes for youth and adults. In 2004, he received the *National Federation for Catholic Youth Ministry* award for Gospel Values of Peace and Justice. Joe lives in inner-city Louisville with his wife and family and is a co-founder of the CrossRoads Ministry retreat center. Joe has authored numerous books and articles on scripture, social justice and spirituality, including a prior volume of reflections entitled *Still In the Storm, Reflections for Engaging Spirituality in times like these.* He maintains a blog entitled *In the Storm Still*: https://engagedpresence.wordpress.com/